John K. Casey

A Wreath of Shamrocks

Ballads, songs and legends

John K. Casey

A Wreath of Shamrocks
Ballads, songs and legends

ISBN/EAN: 9783744792721

Printed in Europe, USA, Canada, Australia, Japan

Cover: Foto ©Thomas Meinert / pixelio.de

More available books at **www.hansebooks.com**

A

WREATH OF SHAMROCKS:

Ballads, Songs, and Legends.

BY

JOHN K. CASEY

(LEO).

"Be blessings on the loved land of my birth!
Where shall I meet with such another?
My nurse—my mother!
The land of lands on earth!"

MANGAN.

DUBLIN:
PUBLISHED BY ROBERT S. M'GEE,
35 LOWER SACKVILLE STREET
(Next the General Post Office).

TO

Y. I.

THIS LITTLE VOLUME IS DEDICATED

BY

THE WRITER.

"Non ille pro caris amicis
Aut patria timidus perire".
    HOR.

Oct. 1, 1866.

BALLADS, SONGS, AND LEGENDS.

THE LAY OF NJAL THE VIKING.

A NORSE LEGEND.

The spring moon looked on our open sails
  As westward away we bore,
And dim in its light paled the rocky face
  Of the gray-browed Nordland shore.

The spectre of midnight wrapped our barque,
  For we heard his low-breathed moan,
And like to a cloud, on the shining deck,
  Our Viking walked alone.

He had laid aside the glittering spear,
  Which led on our battle path;
And his loosened armour creaked like the wind
  That circles the demon's rath.

We knew that a gloom rested on his brow,
    As he paced thus silently;
We knew that his bosom was seething wild,
    As the breakers on the sea.

For Gundolf the seer had read him his fate,
    By the far off hills of snow;
And the prophet's words, by our monarch's looks,
    Were brimmed with a coming woe.

The white stars arose, and in azure sank,
    Full many a time again,
And still we wandered away, away,
    Over the green-lipped main;

Till at length we saw, on the far sea-rim,
    The dark beach of Inisfail,
And our banner fluttered in warlike joy
    As we rushed from the ocean gale.

We brightened our blades, our armour donned,
    And thought of the kine and gold
That our fathers won with their purple blood
    On that rugged coast of old.

Then down to our bark came a minstrel hoar,
    With hair like the wild swan's wing—
"The chieftain, my master, has bid me ask,
    What bringeth thee here, O king?

"If your words speak peace, he has rest to give—
  Food, wassail, and song has he:
If you come in war, he hath shining spears
  And a deadly grasp for thee".

Thus answered our monarch: "Go, tell your chief,
  I want neither food nor rest;
But I want fair Una, the golden haired,
  The maid with the snowy breast.

"I 've a palace home in the northern land,
  And I fain would place her there,
To brighten my soul like a burning star:
  These words unto him now bear".

"Thy coming is late, O strange-tongued king!
  The maid is another's now".
He passed away; and a heavy storm
  Scowled black on our monarch's brow.

The night spread its robes—like a growling bear
  The billows chafed wildly on;
"Where, where is the king?" but none could tell;
  None knew where he was gone.

Our pulses were chill as we reefed the sails,
  And the demon of fire swept past;
We prayed to Thor, for we felt his breath
  In the roaring rush of the blast.

We shook with a dread, such as mortals feel
    When spirits of hell are near;
We quailed as we thought of our absent lord,
    And thought of the words of the seer.

And once in a hush of the storm we heard
    Fierce shouts on the hidden shore,
And a clang of blades; but the sounds were lost,
    And tost in the darkling roar.

The tempest god fled to his hidden cave;
    When the morning sunbeams woke,
We looked to the land,—what a thrilling wail
    From the breasts of our bold crew broke!

For there lay our monarch with shattered crest,
    And the maiden clasp'd in his fold;
We flew to their forms,—but eagle and dove
    Together were dead and cold.

Her ringlets of gold on his bosom slept,
    Where his bravest heart's blood poured,
One hand was around her beautiful form,
    The other hand clutched his sword.

We buried them there in the soft sea sand,
    His mantle their burial shroud;
Full sad was the fate of our wild Viking,
    Of Njal the dauntless and proud.

We buried them there in the lone sea sand,
    And oh! but our looks were dark,
As we shook our sails to the landward breeze,
    And homeward guided our barque.

There was wailing for many and many a day
    On the hills of the snow-robed pine,
For him who went forth to return no more,
    The last of old Harold's line.

There were fearful curses and darksome vows,
    As we told the woeful tale,
How his cairn we raised by the swelling sea,
    On the coast of Inisfail.

MAIRE DONN ASTOR.

Air—*Molly Ban astor.*

In valleys lone I plucked the flowers,
    And wove them in her hair,
And never in the greenwood bowers,
    Looked forest queen as fair.
She gave one silent glance at me,
    With lovelight flowing o'er—
Oh! well that love's returned to thee,
    My Maire Donn Astor.*

    * Brown-haired Mary, my treasure.

The sloethorn woos the poplar brown,
    Where shines the sunlit hill—
Its blossoms waft an odour down
    O'er meadow-slope, and rill.
Her hand is as that blossom white,
    As pure her bosom's core;
My well of joy—my life's delight,
    My Maire Donn Astor.

I've strung my harp to many a lay,
    With soothing magic sound—
I've sung to lords and ladyes gay,
    Throughout old Ireland's ground:
But now I find the tones are vain,
    The ancient songs to pour:
Thy name alone that fills the strain,
    My Maire Donn Astor.

THE WELCOME TO HUGH ROE O'DONNELL.

Oh! welcome back! oh! welcome back unto our hearts once more,—
Hearts joyless, since a captive ta'en, you passed from Ulster's shore;

Oh! welcome back! list to the shouts fierce bursting from the clan,
Who hail the fiery-hearted boy, now risen to a man!

Oh! sorely have we waited thro' the long, slow-footed years,
Still mingling groans and curses with the burning, blinding tears,
Still pining for the avenging march: but now, O'Donnell Roe,
Your bonds are broke, the time has come for vengeance on the foe.

For vengeance on the foe who played the serpent's treacherous part,—
Whose chains pressed down the heavings of our chieftains bounding heart,—
Who kept that spirit lone and dead, which panted for the hills,
The clansman's shout, the creach's song, the crooning of the rills.

The foe whose bloody hand was laid upon Mac Mahon's head,
Who spareth not the living, who disturbeth e'en the dead,

Whose foot blasts all it treads upon, whose cursèd
 flag is dyed
With blood of aged helplessness and boyhood in
 its pride.

And we have marked his hellish path, and trea-
 sured up our hate,
Pile upon pile, we fed the flame, yet still re-
 solved to wait—
Resolved to wait our Hugh's return, for well, oh!
 well we knew
His soul would thirst to grasp a blade, a warrior's
 work to do.

We saw thee in thy dungeon keep count up the
 weary hours,
While paled thy cheek within the shade of those
 sepulchral towers;
We felt the burning of thy soul, as day succeeded
 day,
For green Tirconnell's mountain glens, away, so
 far away.

But NOW, thou 'rt here, as free from thrall as
 eagle in the sky,
And we are here with hand and blade to avenge
 thy wrongs or die;

Thy wrongs, O Hugh! thy country's wrongs, are they remembered now?
We need not ask—the answer rests upon thy clouded brow!

Wilt thou forgive the wily knaves who caught thee in the snare?
Who guarded thee as hunters watch the war wolf in his lair?
What stiffened up the swiftest limbs that ever chased the roe?
Why are those arms so weakly now, that dealt so strong a blow?

Compassion! mercy! will they beam upon thy haughty face?
Aye, when thy steel has pierced the last of all the Saxon race—
When brethren slain with sword and axe return to earth again,
When brave Mac Mahon leads his clan thro' Uriel's mountain glen.

O darling, idol of our hearts! the hour has dawned at last,
O'Neill holds forth the kindly hand, the ancient feud is past;

Come till we crown thee chief upon thy weak-
  souled father's throne,
Then on for Freedom and for Faith, Tirconnell
  and Tireoghain.

There's joy to-night o'er Ulster wide, from Glynn
  to Dunagall,
And merrily wild laughter shakes Dungannon's
  princely hall,
In mountain hut and castle keep bright usque-
  bagh doth flow,
To toast thy health, and welcome back our own
  O'Donnell Roe!

CARROLL BAWN.

1798.

'T was in the town of Wexford
  They sentenced him to die;
'T was in the town of Wexford
  They built the gallows high;
And there one summer morning,
  When beamed the gentle dawn,
Upon that curséd gibbet
  They hung my Carroll Bawn.

Oh! he was true and loyal,
   Oh! he was proud and fair,
And only nineteen summers
   Shone on his golden hair;
And when his gallant brothers
   Had grasped the pike in hand,
Where the green flag streamed the fairest,
   He stood for native land.

I saw him cross the heather,
   With his bold companie,
And from the rising hill side
   He waved his hand to me;
Then on my wild heart settled,
   A load of woe and pain.
Mo bhron! its throbbings told me,
   We'd never meet again.

They fought the Saxon foemen,
   By Slaney's glancing wave;
But brutal strength o'erpowered
   The gallant and the brave:
And in the flight which followed
   That day of misery,
Sore wounded he was taken,
   My Carroll bawn machree.

Oh, *fareer gair!* that ever
  I saw the dreadful sight,
His locks all damply hanging,
  His cheeks so deadly white;
What wonder if my ringlets
  Were changed from dark to gray—
Or if the blessed hand of God
  Had ta'en my life away.

'T was in the town of Wexford
  They sentenced him to die;
'T was in the town of Wexford
  They built the gallows high;
With form erect and manly,
  And look of scornful pride,
For Ireland's faith and freedom
  My true love nobly died.

The meadow path is lonely,
  The hearth is cold and dim,
And the silent churchyard blossom
  Blooms softly over him;
And my heart is ever yearning
  For the calm rest coming on,
When its weary pulse lies sleeping
  Beside my Carroll Bawn.

BY THE SEA.

The soft winds sing across the sea,
   While here I sit, all lone and cold,
Rapt in the rays of memory
   That flash from golden days of old;
For oh! the ocean's murmuring tune
   Speaks to my bosom of a time
When life was as a harvest moon,
   Or warbling of a sylvan rhyme.

An old gray house upon the beach,
   A gentle face that blessed its door
(Whose eyes, like saint's from sculptured niche,
   Look into mine for evermore),
Full voices 'mid the garden flowers,
   To soothe and sanctify the day—
These once were mine, but frozen hours
   Have stolen them all to depths away.

One after one they glided past,
   Borne on the stream that mocks at time,—
On dusty, thorny pathways cast,
   'Mid poisoned cares I lived my prime;
But still the breath of early buds
   Remained to scent the cross I bore,
To give me strength to breast the floods
   That break on life's enclouded shore.

Snow, chilly snow, fell on my way,
   And cast sharp icy thrills around;
But gentle voices, day by day,
   With hopeful tones my faint heart found.
Soft stars looked through the dark-browed skies,
   And poured a pulsing light on me—
I felt they were the radiant eyes
   That lit my youth beside the sea.

Back, Memory! close thy faded leaves,
   And let me ope the page to come;
'T is not with thee my soul now grieves;
   I pine for rest! I thirst for home!
I want to see beloved forms,
   I want to clasp soft hands again,
To hear no more the roaring storms,
   To feel no more the aching pain.

FRANCES.

Air—*The Coulin.*

Oh! it is not the ringlets that stream from her brow,
Nor the neck and soft hand which outrival the snow,
Nor the lips like the fruit of the tall apple-tree,
That make my sweet Frances so dear unto me.

Oh! it is not the music that flows from her
  mouth
When she sings the soft lays of her own native
  South,
Nor the flash from her eyes, like the moon on
  Glanree,
That makes my sweet Frances so dear unto me.

But a grace and a charm that are lovelier still—
'T is the soul shining pure as the snow on the
  hill,
'T is the heart beating true as the waves on the
  sea,
That make my sweet Frances so dear unto me.

She is proud as the eagle on Mangerton's crest,
Yet gentle as dove brooding o'er her young nest,
With a pulse throbbing high for the cause of the
  free—
And this makes my Frances so dear unto me.

How oft have we rambled the dear mountain
  path,
And plucked the white blossoms beside the old
  rath,
And I plaited a wreath for my *cushla machree*,
And whispered that she was the dearest to me.

Then I told her the tales of the grand days of
  old,
Of the ladies so bright, and the chieftains so
  bold,
Till she sighed for the fall of the gallant and
  free—
And this made her dearer, far dearer to me.

Oh! years may go by with their sunshine and
  rain,
With the light clouds of joy, and the dark ones of
  pain,
But true, as my heart pulse, where'er I may
  be,
My Frances *astor* will be dearest to me.

—◦◦—

THE OUTCAST ONE.

Mirth was in that distant city on a mellow sum-
    mer even,
  Sounds of laughter and of music float along
    the twilight air,
Down the fragrant moonlight streameth from the
    azure cheeks of heaven,
  And the stars in stilness glitter with a light
    divinely fair.

Laughter on the crowded footway, where the
   slaves of fashion wander—
   Laughter in the shaded gardens and the tall-
   browed palace hall—
Laughter—ha! what spectral figure crouches in
   the shadows yonder?
   What's that object, fairest lady, leaning 'gainst
   thy trellised wall?

There's a cold sneer on her lip, and her jewelled
   brow is arching
   With the scorn of a spirit that mocks at human
   woe,
And her eyes gaze on unheeding at the myriads
   thickly marching:
   Ay, that wretched outcast beggar—what of her
   has she to know?

She is flesh and blood—what say you? Thou
   hast riches, rank, and splendour,
   Servants bowing to thy bidding, proud ones
   kneeling at thy feet;
Soft that mantle on thy shoulders, and thy
   cushioned seat is tender;
   Then what care you for a sister lying starving
   in the street?

Ten, eleven—how the hours pass away—like
  flashes flying,
 Where the devil holds the doorway, holds the
  password, and the key!
Ten, eleven!—ah! how slowly to that gentle
  maiden dying!
 None to fling the dew of pity on her frenzied
  agony.

Twelve! A tramp upon the side-path—"Off,
  away! no place for sleeping—
 Off, away!" the watchman crieth in the calm-
  ness of the night;
And she totters slowly, weakly, with her eyelids
  scorched with weeping,
 And a brow of whiter marble never faced the
  broad moonlight!

I have seen that brow of marble in a glow of
  health and beauty,
 Where the Shannon ripples softly by the tow-
  ers of Athlone,
Where the tall hills nurse the streamlets with a
  mother's love and duty,
 As they wander ever plashing over beds of
  amber stone.

And those eyes, now red and burning, then were
    kindly, soft, and loving;
And those brown locks danced as freely as the
    breeze that shook them free;
And those feet tripped o'er the heather swiftly
    as the young hare roving;
And those pale lips were the reddest from that
    river to the sea.

But a cloud spread o'er the landscape, and a
    hearth in desolation
Echoed back the farewell parting of its last,
    last tenant gone:
She was parted from the lone graves of her kin-
    dred and her nation—
Like a waif she drifted onward, in a stranger
    land, alone.

*   *   *   *   *   *   *

Tell no tales, O dismal river! do not whisper
    out *that* story:
Oh! that story! that dark story! hush it in
    thy deepest wave,
Or the mother that once nursed her, and the
    father old and hoary,
Would arise to curse thy waters from the low
    depths of the grave.

Still the palace hall is laden with its freight of
    gold and pearl,
Still the jewelled lady gazeth with a haughty
    look of pride;
While the broken-hearted outcast, that weak,
    starving Irish girl,
Floats away unto the ocean on the river's
    moonlit tide.

MAIRE MY GIRL.

Air—*Mairgread ni Chealleadh.*

Over the dim blue hills
    Strays a wild river,
Over the dim blue hills
    Rests my heart ever.
Dearer and brighter than
    Jewels and pearl,
Dwells she in beauty there,
    Maire my girl.

Down upon Claris heath
    Shines the soft berry,
On the brown harvest tree
    Droops the red cherry.

Sweeter thy honey lips,
   Softer the curl
Straying adown thy cheeks,
   Maire my girl.

'T was on an April eve
   That I first met her;
Many an eve shall pass
   Ere I forget her.
Since, my young heart has been
   Wrapped in a whirl,
Thinking and dreaming of
   Maire my girl.

She is too kind and fond
   Ever to grieve me,
She has too pure a heart
   E'er to deceive me.
Were I Tyrconnell's chief
   Or Desmond's earl,
Life would be dark, wanting
   Maire my girl.

Over the dim blue hills
   Strays a wild river,
Over the dim blue hills
   Rests my heart ever;

Dearer and brighter than
　　Jewels or pearl,
Dwells she in beauty there,
　　Maire my girl!

THE REAPER OF GLANREE.

We sat around the fireside—'t was in the Christmas time—
And lightly passed the hours away with story, song, and rhyme;
But of the wild old legends blind Fergus told to me
None set my young heart bounding like the Reaper of Glanree.

"'T is sixty-four long summers since the days of '98—
Black days of desolation, of murder, and of hate—
The truest and the bravest, then, in all the counterie,
Was dashing Gerald Murtagh, the Reaper of Glanree.

"As brown as autumn chesnuts his ranting, roving eye,
His form a mountain-ash tree, so towering, strong, and high;
An arm of tempered iron, a voice of jovial glee,
And a soul as clear as diamond, had the Reaper of Glanree.

"Bright morning on the moorland and hillside soft and green,
But at his daily labour young Gerald is not seen;
His hook lies on the hurdle, 'just where it ought to be,
When pikes cut down the harvest', said the Reaper of Glanree.

"'Your mother weeps all lonely, your father's gray with grief,
And Cathaleen O'Reilly is gone past all relief'.
'Oh! go and bring them kindly this message now from me—
My country is my true love', said the Reaper of Glanree.

"The yeomen mustered strongly, a lawless, bloody crew;
His pikemen, stout and gallant, bold Gerald mustered too;

In on the foemen's vanguard they charged with
    fearless glee—
'Old *Faing an lea* for ever!' cried the Reaper of
    Glanree.

"The Saxon bay'nets beaten, they tried the
    yellow gold,
And Gerald and his sweetheart were treacher-
    ously sold;
Full hotly did they chase him through Meath
    and Annalee,
But a match for spy and soldier was the Reaper of
    Glanree.

"'Cold in the clay they're lying, my parents,
    side by side,
And Cathaleen O'Reilly a mongrel traitor's bride;
But still, oh! still, my country! I pledge my
    troth to thee;
You never will deceive me', said the Reaper of
    Glanree.

"The stars were sweetly shining on Longford's
    ancient town;
The sentry's eyes were seeking the Camlen waters
    brown—

A tap upon his shoulder—'What do you want
of me?'
'Och! nothing but a lodging; I'm the Reaper
of Glanree'.

"Right safely did they lodge him until the com-
ing day,
And stern and short the sentence—'Death! death
without delay'.
With foot upon the gallows, eyes flashing fear-
lessly,
And a cheer for faith and country, died the
Reaper of Glanree".

And thus blind Fergus chanted, at holy Christ-
mas time,
His brave and noble story, in rough, untutored
rhyme;
And oft I cried, "Dear Erinn! this heart now
vows to thee
A love as pure and faithful as the Reaper's of
Glanree".

GOLDSMITH

BY THE LOIRE.*

The calm air rested on the grass
   Brown-hued by summer's fading sun,
   And far above the vapours dun
Were clustering in a fleecy mass.

From trellised doors low drooped the vine,
   And sounds of soft Provençal song
   Rose from the happy peasant throng
A-quaffing draughts of fragrant wine.

Far sunward, like a band of gold,
   The broad Loire gleamed bright and fair,
   As when, with stout spears bristling, there
The Norman Roú his flag unrolled.

A silence holds the merry crowd
   As upward, from the dusty way,
   A traveller cometh—strange to say,
A traveller poor, yet stepping proud.

His face has not the Gallic hue,
   Around his lips there plays a smile
   Like one whose breast is free from guile,
To God and nature firm and true.

* Suggested by a view of his statuette in Ballymahon Reading Room.

"Here, here is peace, yet not for me,
    Let me enjoy it while I may,
    I yearn for other scenes away
In my own land across the sea".

The wanderer sits before the door
    Amid that eager, wondering band,
    The wine cup in his claspèd hand,
Before him spread the household store.

He thinks how long he pined and pined
    The world and all its shades to see,
    Its "Citizen" alone to be—
And here is what his heart divined.

Yet there is something wanting still—
    The mother's love, the father's prayer,
    The freshness of his native air,
The ancient home, the rath-crowned hill.

This is the void—but now the rays
    Of moonlight kiss the ripening fruit;
    He breathes into his soft-tuned flute,
And young eyes fill the while he plays.

The sad old tunes that soothe his breast
    Along the air in richness flow,
    Freighted with dreams of long ago,
Dreams full of pearls and silken rest.

A change! a change! the jovial strain—
   Old Ballymahon town appears;
   "Bob", "Jack", and all the wild compeers
Of awkward, mad brained "Noll" again!

As swiftly round the dancers go,
   He thinks he rides on "Fiddleback",
   The careless poet's sorry hack,
With spirits in congenial flow.

Thus 'neath the smiling moon of France
   He laughs and plays his melodies
   To thoughts and fancies such as these,
That through his brain in madness dance.

So be it. Let the scoffer sneer—
   Goldsmith! thy life is understood
   By all, like thee, who love the good,
To whom God's work is always dear.

Thy follies! we can let them pass,
   And make the bright lights ever shine
   That sparkle from a soul divine
As clear and pure as crystal glass.

The traveller now, the preacher then—
   The poet-preacher filled with love,
   As gentle as the light above
That woos the rugged hearts of men.

Here, in the spot thy feet oft pressed,
  A Celtic minstrel tribute pays
  To all thy strange and generous ways,
Thy faults, thy virtues, and the rest.

Peace to thy clay! Let other men
  Chant forth thy fame in golden song;
  I stand and ask, among the throng,
Where will thy like be found again?

THE BIRD AND THE LADYE.

A little bird sat on a bough
  While drearily the snow was falling;
Its eye was dark, its breast was red,
And lowly drooped its crested head
  Before the wind so wildly calling.
Full sad it sung a mournful lay
  Down i' that silent forest glen:
"My merry mate is gone away;
  Oh! when will he return again?
My merry mate is gone away;
  When, when will he return again?"

A ladye at her window leant,
  Her brown hair on her shoulders straying;
She looked across the misty hills,
And listened to the bursting rills
  That fiercely laughed, like giants playing;
And thus the snow-wind bore the lay
  Adown the lonely mountain glen:
"My true love, he is gone away;
  Oh! when will he return again?
My true love, he is gone away;
  When, when will he return again?"

The Spring light kissed Slieve Carn's brow,
  And bright the "silver dew" was falling;
Right merrilie a little bird
Down i' the lonely wood was heard
  Among the budding flowerets calling:
"The cold, cold snow has fled away
  From hillside green and forest glen,
And Spring has brought the evenings gay,
  And brought my true mate back again;
Oh! Spring has brought the mornings gay,
  And brought my true mate back again".

And down beside the castle wall,
  Where Inny's wave was softly playing,
A noble knight, with plume of green,
And gentlest ladye, might be seen

Across the daisied meadows straying.
They sat beneath an ash-tree gray,
And thus her voice flowed down the glen:
"The Spring has brought the flowerets gay,
And brought my true love back again;
Oh! Spring has brought the flowerets gay,
And brought my true love home again".

THE RISING OF THE MOON.

A.D. 1798.

Air—*The Wearing of the Green.*

"Oh! then tell me, Shawn O'Ferrall,
Tell me why you hurry so?"
"Hush, ma bouchal, hush and listen",
And his cheeks were all a-glow.
"I bear ordhers from the captain,
Get you ready quick and soon,
For the pikes must be together
At the risin' of the moon".

"Oh! then tell me, Shawn O'Ferrall
Where the gatherin' is to be?"
"In the ould spot by the river,
Right well known to you and me.

One word more—for signal token
   Whistle up the marchin' tune,
With your pike upon your shoulder,
   By the risin' of the moon".

Out from many a mudwall cabin
   Eyes were watching thro' that night,
Many a manly chest was throbbing
   For the blessed warning light.
Murmurs passed along the valleys
   Like the banshee's lonely croon,
And a thousand blades were flashing
   At the risin' of the moon.

There beside the singing river
   That dark mass of men was seen,
Far above the shining weapons
   Hung their own beloved green.
"Death to ev'ry foe and traitor!
   Forward! strike the marchin' tune,
And hurrah, my boys, for freedom!
   'T is the risin' of the moon".

Well they fought for poor old Ireland,
   And full bitter was their fate
(Oh! what glorious pride and sorrow
   Fill the name of Ninety-Eight).

Yet, thank God, e'en still are beating
Hearts in manhood's burning noon,
Who would follow in their footsteps
At the risin' of the moon!

CHRISTMAS MEMORIES.

Oh! those Christmas times, mavourneen, are not like the times of old,
When the light of love shone softly, and our pulses felt no cold;
When the laughter of the young hearts round the hearth rang merrily;—
Now the laughter and the young hearts all are gone, asthore, machree!

Methinks I see our darling Kate, her blue eyes fixed on mine,
And dark haired Patrick resting soft his little hand in mine;
Methinks I hear brave Owen's voice, and Brian's free and gay,
With soft cheeked Eily's mingling in the holy Christmas lay.

Dreams! dreams! to-night the ancient hearth no
  kindly look doth wear,
There is snow upon the threshold stone and chill-
  ness everywhere.
No swell of rushing voices pours the holy
  Christmas lay,
The young hearts, and the merry hearts, ma-
  vourneen, where are they?

Ah, blue-eyed Kate and Patrick Dhu, long, long
  have found their rest,
Where Shruel's silent churchyard looks across
  the Inny's breast;
And, Eily, thy young heart lies cold and pulseless
  'neath the sea
Full many and many a Christmas-tide, alanna
  bawn machree.

And by Potómac's blood-tinged wave brave Owen
  nobly fell.
My gallant boy! they say he fought right glo-
  riously and well;
And Brian's voice is hushed in death, where blue
  Australian streams
Fill with their youthful melodies the exile's glow-
  ing dreams.

Asthore, asthore, beside the light our faces shine alone;
But they are clustered with the stars before the eternal throne:
With St. Patrick and St. Brigid and the angels robed in white,
They sing the old remembered strains, their Christmas hymn, to-night.

Old love! old love! His will be blessed that left e'en you to me
To keep my heart from bursting with the wild, wild memory.
That soothing glance, mavourneen, speaks of Christmas times to come,
When the scattered hearts shall meet for aye in God's eternal home.

—◦◦—

AUTUMN SONNETS.

I.—THE HARVEST MOON.

Amid a sea of radiance, glorious Moon!
  Thou wand'rest onward, dreamless, changeless still—

Oh! let my spirit now with thee commune,
   And of thy raptured splendour quaff its fill,
   Till mingles with thy silence every ill,
Till care forgets its missioned task, and dies,
And weary, wasting sorrow swiftly flies
   Adown the current of oblivion's rill.
Oh! let the flood of light which crowns thee now,
   Upon my sinking soul pour down a dew
   To smoothe the hollow wrinkles on my brow,
And make life's dusty garment fresh and new:
Thus born again in boyhood's bursting noon,
My soul will walk with thee, O glorious Moon!

II.—REAPING.

Reap on, ye stricken hearts—weak hands, reap on!
   The glowing sheaf beneath your strokes must lie,
Albeit the blood within your veins runs dry,
Albeit the hue that lit your cheeks is gone:
   What recks the stranger of your burning toil?
   What cares he if your sweat bedew the soil?
Your lives are his—his labour must be done.
Oh! lift not to the sky your faces pale!
   Poor slaves! ye would not hold what heaven gave;

Ye trembled at the rising of the gale—
  Ye feared to stand before the surging wave—
Ye feared to claim your own : reap on, reap on!
God, in good time, stout hearts and hands will send,
Who 'll sow, and reap, and hold His treasures to the end.

THE CHANGE.

I saw her in her country home,
    Near brown Slieve Bán,
With brow as white as ocean foam,
    Face like the dawn,
And lips that rivalled in their hue
  The berry on the heathy moor,
And eyes like shining drops of dew,
  And heart as pure.

I saw her in her city home,
    Sad, worn, and wan;
And then I asked, "why did she roam
    From far Slieve Bán?"
Ah! paler grew her sunken cheek,
  And darker shadows dimmed her brow,
As she essāyed the words to speak,
  "I 'm homeless now".

"The tyrant's minions fiercely came
  Unto our cot,
And soon the rafter's lurid flame
  Illumed the spot.
My father died—my friends were fled,
 Poor exiles, o'er the frothing sea—
And I came here to toil for bread
  In misery.

"Still toiling on in scathing woe
  From day to day;
Within my breast no hopeful glow
  To light my way;
Unknown I walk among the crowd,
 Without a smile, without a word,
To cheer a spirit downward bowed,
  Long pierced and gored.

"Oh! if I could but see once more
  Slieve Bán's dark crest,
Or hear the waves at evening roar
  On Shannon's breast,
The healthful flush might fill my cheek,
 And chase the aching from my brow.
Movrone! movrone! why do I speak?—
  I'm homeless now".

THE HORSEMAN OF DUNRONE.

A NINETY-EIGHT BALLAD.

PART I.

"Rise up! rise up! O'Brennan Roe, as quickly as you may,
Or else you lie in fetters bound before the break of day;
Rise up! rise up! the redcoats now are marching from Athy,
And the captain of the bloody horde has sworn that you must die".

He leaped unto the window, but the warning voice was gone;
His hand upon his carbine laid, his garments hurried on,
He kissed his sleeping brother's brow, and hastened out with speed,
And soon was riding o'er the plain upon his gallant steed.

The moonlight fell in golden streams across the waving heath,
And brightly looked each little star upon the earth beneath;

No sound was on the night-wind, save the Bar-
    row's lonely fall,
And the whistling of the plover mingled with the
    grouse's call.

"On, on, brave horse! your mission now is life
    or death to me!
To-night, to-bid a long farewell, my true love I
    must see.
To-morrow! then, ye Saxon dogs! come seize
    me, if you dare!
My faith! but ye shall rue the day ye marched
    into Kildare!"

He rode away, he rode away, o'er grassy bawn
    and moor,
And ne'er checked rein until he stood before his
    true love's door;
A gentle tap and whisper, and the door was
    opened wide,
And Brigid Bawn O'Heffernan was clinging to
    his side.

Oh! tremblingly she listened to the tidings he
    did tell,
And on his brave and manly heart her tears in
    torrents fell;

He thought to soothe the heavy grief—but all his words were vain,
For he felt himself the shadow of a coming cloud of pain.

"They 've tracked me now, *acushla!* they are thirsting for my life,
But to-morrow I shall meet them breast to breast in deadly strife,
And the eagle on the battle-field will pick a dainty fare
In the fat and pampered tyrants of the county of Kildare.

"And won't your eyes flash brightly when our conq'ring bands are seen,
With their weapons all a-shining, and old Erin's flag of green!
Then hush! and dry those tears away—'t is time that we should part".
He flung his arms around her, and he pressed her to his heart.

Her hair in wild disorder lay in tresses on his cheek,
And neither in those moments sad the parting words could speak;—

But the silent clasp was broken by a wild and
  shrilly neigh,
And wildly was it answered but a meadow's
  length away.

There is a tramping and a clanking—'t is the
  march of the dragoon—
And a score of helmets gleaming in the full blaze
  of the moon;
"They 're here! they 're here! quick, darling,
  quick! you 're lost, if you are seen!"
A leap into the saddle, and he sweeps across the
  green.

He rode away, he dashed away, by grassy bawn
  and moor,
But the bright moon led the foemen on as swiftly
  and as sure;
Yet, though deadly was his peril, still there lay
  upon his mind
A heavier load of sorrow for his true love left
  behind.

He rode away, he rode away, and gallantly his
  steed
Showed the mettle which is ever found the true
  man's friend at need;

O'er field and ditch and road and stream, o'er
  bog and sluggish fen,
Till he gained the guarded trysting of the brave
  United Men.

What a shout of manly greeting met the weary
  rider there,
As he leaped into the centre of the heroes of
  Kildare!
"The chase was hot to-night, my boys—the
  quarry's still at bay;
But the bloodhounds on another track will curse
  the rising day".

PART II.

The morning sun was peeping softly through the
  dawning cloud,
And its rays were flowing brightly on a dark and
  massy crowd—
It fell upon a forest of bright pikes in warlike
  sheen,
That were glinting on the hill-top 'neath the flag
  of gold and green.

And up the dewy heather bands of men were
  marching on,

All pouring like a thousand streams to where
  that banner shone;
And riding here, and riding there, with hanging
  bridal rein,
Frieze-coated horsemen guarded all the toghers*
  to the plain.

Anon a group with laughter hoarse were sharp-
  ening their blades,
And others tying in their hats the flashing green
  cockades;
But one among that multitude stood silently alone:
'T was Patrick Roe O'Brennan, the young horse-
  man of Dunrone.

"O'Brennan!" — 't was his kinsman spoke —
  O'Ryan, stout and true —
"No time it is for thinking when there's heavy
  work to do.
'T was my voice that gave you warning of the
  wily Saxon foe,
And now I bear you tidings it is well that you
  should know.

"Last night I lay in ambush hid, and saw a sight
  that well
Might raise the deepest envy of the demons down
  in hell:

* Roads.

Boy! listen till your heart's blood boils and
blazes with revenge—
*You 've a mother and a brother and a sweetheart to
avenge.*

" Your mother and your brother in the burning
thatch were flung,
And by her glossy yellow hair your Brigid Og
was hung;
Your name was last upon her lips, when, through
her torn vest,
The sword of cursed Captain Gore was sheathed
in her breast.

" God! have I not the same sight seen—the same
red woes withstood—
When I found my hearthstone clotted with my
murdered parents' blood?
When I found my wife and children swinging
naked on a tree?"—
But the listener's face was whiter than the snow
upon the lea.

And for a moment seemed he just as if the life
were fled,
And his eyes glared in their sockets with the
cold stare of the dead;

The bridle fell down from his grasp—he gave a heavy groan—
Then again his frame grew steady and as silent as a stone.

He flung himself upon the sod, he looked up in the air—
A cross from out his bosom drew, now heaving broad and bare;
A tear fell on the holy sign—his comrade's hand he took—
"Sleeps she in holy earth?" he cried, with stern, unbending look.

"Yes, yes—at dawning of the light I placed her in the grave,
Beside the old brown abbey wall o'erlooking Barrow's wave".
"Thank God!—and now my murdered kin, my outraged, butchered love,
I swear to have red blood for blood, by Him who reigns above!

"I swear to hunt your murderers, by night and open day,
Until their blood smokes in the air as thick as ocean spray".

He kissed the cross, then backed his horse, his carbine slinging free:
"For vengeance and old Ireland, true hearts! now follow me".

On many a field that voice was heard—that carbine's ringing sound—
And many a redcoat fierce and tall his *scian* struck to the ground;
The first to rush upon the foe, and ever last to fly,
Well might the Saxons tremble when they heard his charging cry.

* * * * * *

A small and weary band of men, unconquered to the last,
With tall pikes clutched in grim despair, across the borders passed:
Brave hearts! through hosts of enemies they 've cut their way alone,
And foremost rides O'Brennan Roe, the horseman of Dunrone.

All, all around the bayonets close—a grim, unbroken wall—
And feebler still the heroes strike, as one by one they fall;

A single rider falls the last—yet, ere he ceased
   to breathe,
His murdered love was well avenged on the corn
   slopes of Meath.

―○○―

THE HILLS OF CONNEMARA.

The night-mist thickens o'er the town,
   The twilight's paling dimmer,
A-through the chill, hum-laden air
   The gaslights faintly glimmer.
In exile here I sit and think,
   My heart surcharged with sorrow,
Of home, and friends that watch for me
      On the hills of Connemara—
         Those glorious hills!
         Those kindly hills!
      The hills of Connemara.

The night-mist thickens o'er the town,
   But heavier mists are falling
On the Irish breast, bereft of love,
   For peace and rest long calling.

Alone! alone! where millions throng,
  As if my brain to harrow
With golden dreams of thundering streams
    On the hills of Connemara—
      The loving hills,
      The wild-eyed hills,
    The hills of Connemara.

On Corrib's cheeks the moonlight sleeps,
  The currach skims full lightly;
O'er Clifden's slopes our mountain girls
  Now wander singing blithely,
And I must bear this strife and din,
  While memory strives to borrow
One look of love, one sparkling glance
    Of the hills of Connemara.
      O soft-faced hills!
      O brown-tipped hills—
    Brave hills of Connemara!

God's dearest blessing dwell with them;
  God bless the race they foster,
If Ireland's sons were all as true,
  We never would have lost her.
God prosper all my burning hopes,
  The hopes to crown to-morrow,
When the streams will sing my welcome back

To the hills of Connemara,—
   My native hills,
   My childhood's hills,
The hills of Connemara!

BOUCHALEEN DHOUN.

My true love he dwells on the mountains,
   Like a war-eagle fearless and free,
By the side of the low-tuning fountains
   That wander through wide Annalee.
His soul has more valour and honour
   Than a king with a palace and crown,
For the blood of the race of O'Connor
   Fills the veins of my *Bouchaleen Dhoun*.

Soft *cead mille failte* I give him
   When he comes ev'ry Sunday to me,
And what can I do but believe him
   As he whispers *acushla machree?*
For the look is so truthful and tender
   Of his bright roving eyes of dark brown,
That I'm sure e'en a lady in splendour
   Would be coaxed by my *Bouchaleen Dhoun*.

My father has riches in plenty,
   And suitors for me in his eye;
But, oh! let my age come to twenty—
   If I don't give them all the good-bye!
For I sigh for a life on the mountains
   Far away from the dust of the town,
With the song of the soft-tuning fountains
   And the love of my *Bouchaleen Dhoun.*

DESPAIR NOT.

Think of the past—do not despair,
Nor fill with useless sighs the air;
But grasp the flag with steady will,
And firm as rock upon a hill.
Read ye the lesson taught of old
By those who now lie dark and cold,
The gallant hearts who lost the crown,
Yet never bowed the spirit down.

They saw the dawning pale and fade,
The deadly havoc tempests made;
But love shone pure, and faith was bright,
The twin-stars of their clouded night.

Again they front the tyrant-mass,
Again they 're strewed like tedded grass,
Yet conquerors, for they left behind
The trophies of a country's mind.

Despair not! blazon forth this scroll
Upon thy country's bannered roll:
The righteous cause can never bend
Until it conquers in the end.
What though the chieftains all are gone!
A line of chiefs still cometh on
To send the cry from sea to sea—
We must be free!—we must be free!

THE POET.

A MIDNIGHT GLANCE.

The gray haze floats across the moon,
   The white stars through the depths look down,
While gently broods the soft night noon
   Over the ancient sea-fringed town.
Another light is shining there
So weirdlike in the stilly air,
As if to mock with ghastly glare
   The gems that stud the Heavens' broad crown.

Hushed is the busy, fev'rish din
That filled the ear the whole day long.
Hushed is the trilling violin,
The wandering singer's twilight song;
And by that light low bendeth one
Who seemeth as if all were gone,
And he a watcher in the gloom,
The midnight sentry of the tomb,
Or gaunt and pulseless skeleton,
To haunt that narrow, cheerless room.

But nineteen summers cast a hue
Within those dreaming eyes of blue;
Yet settled woe has left a trace
Upon the brow and flushing face.
Loveless and friendless, there he sits,
Amid his old and treasured books,
As minute after minute flits,
His manly forehead closer knits
Above the page with anxious looks,
Tracing away with rapid thought
The burning dreams his brain has wrought—
Dead, dead to all save that wild song
That, like a broad stream, rolls along,
Bearing away the leaves that were,
Ere friendship left the sting of care,
Ere love came on all starred with gold,
To find him young, and leave him old.

The song must come, though passion's well
　Is dried to vapour at its source,—
Although it cometh but to tell
　How destiny can pave a course.
So let him sing. The haunted noon
Shall bear it calmly to the moon,
Till spirits of the dead will glide
In close communion to his side,
And whisper in a soothing strain,
Thou shalt not live and work in vain.

The glaring lamp is quenched, and cool
　The moonlight sleeps upon his brow,
He leans his head upon his hand,
And thinks of that bright spirit land
Where God alone doth teach and rule,
　Where they are resting happy now :
And, ere the pale stars seek the sea,
　To bathe their cheeks in crested foam,
His soul forgets the woe and dree
　A-dreaming of that far-off home.

SONG OF GOLDEN-HEADED NIAMH.

AN OSSIANIC LAY.

Oh! come with me to Tirnan-og;
There fruit and blossoms bend each tree,
Red sparkling wine and honey flow,
And beauty smiles from sea to sea.
Your flowing locks will ne'er turn gray,
No wrinkles on your forehead come,
Nor burning pain nor grim decay,
Across the threshold of your home.
 So haste away to Tirnan-og,
  My white steed waits in golden sheen;
  A diadem shall crown thy brow,
  And I will be thy bridal queen.

The feast is spread, within the hall
 Flash drinking cups with gold encrowned;
The harp leans lightly 'gainst the wall
 To strike for thee the welcome sound.
A hundred sword-blades for thy hand,
 A hundred of the swiftest steeds,
A hundred hounds, a matchless band
 Where'er the hunted quarry leads.

So haste away to Tirnan-og,
  My white steed waits in golden sheen;
A diadem shall crown thy brow,
  And I will be thy bridal queen.

A hundred robes of precious silk,
  And gems from an enchanted mine,
A hundred kine of sweetest milk,
  And armour of the brightest shine.
And thou shalt wear that wondrous sword
  Of keenest edge, whose flash is death:
The summer wind will hear thy word,
  And gently pour its tender breath.
    So haste away to Tirnan-og,
      My white steed waits in golden sheen;
    A diadem shall crown thy brow,
      And I will be thy bridal queen.

Young virgins, sweetest in the song,
  And beauteous as the morning sun,
Around thy noble steps will throng
  To make thy path a joyous one;
And heroes, in the combat stern,
  In speed and boldness unsurpassed,
Before whose prowess Fionn would learn
  To bow his haughty head at last.
    So haste away to Tirnan-og:
      My white steed waits in golden sheen;

A diadem shall crown thy brow,
And I will be thy bridal queen.

O Oisin of the powerful hand!
  First in the chase, first in the war,
Over our sweet and glorious land
  Thy gallant deeds were borne afar.
Loch Leine is deep, but deeper still
  In Niamh's soul thy image dwells;
Then turn thee westward from this hill
  To where the sun-hued billow swells.
    Oh! haste away to Tirnan-og;
      My white steed waits in golden sheen;
    A diadem will crown thy brow,
      And I will be thy bridal queen.

PARTED.

We met when April clouds with softened bloom
  Were floating o'er the orchard and the hill:
We parted when spring visions sought the tomb,
  And summer voices murmured in each rill.

The cowslips glittered on the pastures fair,—
  We wandered onward, but we saw them not;
I twined my fingers through my darling's hair,
  And in her eyes divined my future lot.

We saw but one another, and the time
   Sailed on as leaves upon an open stream.
Our hearts were pulsing in a gentle rhyme,
   Our faces lit with an ethereal gleam.

The heather lapse stretched into fairy land,
   Far off where shone a low and lonely star:
We joined the spirits of that radiant band,
   Nor saw the tempest coming from afar.

It burst! a flash—a rending of the skies—
   A blinding phantom on our vision crost.
It passed! the light into the distance dies:
   I stood alone: my treasured love was lost.

Lost! lost! and nevermore, oh! nevermore
   To stand beside me in the light of love,
To whisper stories of that beauteous shore
   With accents softer than the cooing dove.

Oh! nevermore; and yet, while twilight falls,
   I sit alone in weariness and pain,
A voice amid the fading vapour calls—
   I think I see that olden face again.

TO CHARLES J. KICKHAM.

The winter moon shines down on Slieve-na-mon,
    Crowning with light its misty crest of blue;
The Christmas snow from upland slopes is gone;
    The tranquil air weeps down a silvery dew.
Oh! why this grief by Anner's flowery side,
    And far across old Munster's hill-girt plain?
Mobhrōn! mobhrōn! bold Tipperary's pride
    Is wearing now the Saxon's felon chain—
The chain our fathers strove to burst, and strove
    in vain.

Art thou a felon, then, O child of song!
    Brave singer, true to Erin's grief of years?
Art thou a felon, while the hireling throng
    Of heartless traitors trace anew their tears?
O God! again we see the informer's brow,
    The fiendish sneer upon his branded face;
Again the burning love and changeless vow,
    And stainless glory of the brave old race,—
The patriots, one by one, stand in their fathers'
    place.

The eagle on the cliff can proudly soar;
    The eagle in the cage, though spirit-bowed,
Still bears the warlike front he ever bore
    As changeless as when rushing through the cloud.
Fetters are clasped upon the patriot's hand,
    But say what fetters hold they for the mind;
Have they a chain within our darkened land
    The Celtic love of liberty to bind,
The legacy and trust our fathers left behind?

They chain the noble-minded, pure, and true;
    They place the minstrel in the murderer's cell,
Where frame and soul that once in glory grew
    Must feel the tortures of a second hell.
The bard who sang of Irish truth and love,
    And feasted on his country's golden page,
Whose heart is gentle as a woodland dove,
    Now bends before a brutal gaoler's rage,
Because the ancient war of right he dared to wage.

And shall we curse them in our bursting wrath?
    Look at that face, so sad, resigned, and wan:
That heart now dreams of childhood's flowery path,
    Of Anner's stream, and glorious Slievenamon.

Charles, farewell! the bolts grate on my ear:
As Tasso suffered for his proud love's sake,
A felon's chain for Ireland now you wear,
    Yet be of cheer,—let not your brave heart break,—
For yet this sleeping land in Freedom's light shall wake.

A VISION OF THE HEARTH.

Ghostly through the chilly ether
    Glides the silent, cheerless snow,
And the wind across the heather
    Growls and mutters deep and low;
Dimmer burns the wasting fire,
    Lower droops its ruddy blaze,
And as spark and spark expire,
    Sadder, wearier, I gaze.

For I see in every ember
    Some beloved departed face
That my heart would fain remember,
    And my eye essay to trace.
But like airy sprites they vanish,
    Shadowed forth, and swiftly gone,
And their memories all I banish,
    All except one darling one.

She, the angel of my morning,
   Noontide softly stole away,
Now a brighter land adorning,
   Blooming in the eternal day.
But she left a bosom lonely,
   Cold with grief, and dark with woe,
Withered, pulseless, waiting only
   For the destined time to go.

Ah! to-night I feel the sorrow
   Of a heart that is alone,
And in vain I try to borrow
   Soothing from the tempest's moan.
Vain! from every object fading,
   She doth sadly gaze at me,
And a soft face fills the shading
   That is formed by memory.

Sadder, paler, shows the vision;
   Fainter shines the embers' glow;
Slowly now that face Elysian
   Glides away like passing snow—
Glides away, and leaves me mourning
   In the silence of the room,
While the last faint ember burning
   Sickly lights the eerie gloom.

Outside still the snow is falling;
  Inside is a heart as cold,
All the latent joys recalling
  That illumed in days of old.
Still recalling, yet not bringing
  Light or hope or peace to me,
But a quenchless sorrow clinging
  Ever to their memory.

WHEN COOL WINDS ARE BLOWING.

When cool winds are blowing, I love to be rowing
  My merry boat down to where sweet Gracie dwells,
When the forests are ringing with laughter and singing,
  And sweet briers scent Ballymulvy's lone dells.
The blue leaping river I'd sail on for ever
  To catch the fresh light of my *cailín's* young face
And yellow locks shining, with white lilies twining,
  Their splendour encrowning with beauty and grace.

How pleasant to meet her, how joyous to greet her,
   Her lips flushing soft as she welcomes me in;
The wheel ever humming soon stops at my coming,
   For Gracie gets weary of trying to spin.
We sit in the bower beside the gray tower,
   Where the tall beechen trees whisper tales to the moon.
Such bright dreams they bring me, the sweet lays she sings me,
   That my poor throbbing heart beats in time to the tune.

A-down the blue river my boat's sailing ever,
   Since we lit the *bealtin* on the eve of St. John.
We joined in the sporting, the dancing and courting—
   My young heart was stolen, and Gracie's I won.
That night I was dreaming, with fairy-like seeming,
   I sat on the gray walls by Inny's green side:
The music was sounding, the dancers were bounding,
   And Gracie beside me, my own wedded bride.

Oh! if some kind fairy, on wings free and airy,
   Would steal her away to my home on the hill,

I 'd hide in my bosom my tender young blossom,
  As the ash-tree the violet by Shaskan's dark
    rill.
When the evening shades quiver, we 'd sail down
    the river,
  By the old mossy weir where flossy crests run,
And the gloom of the winter no longer could
    enter
  The hearth that was blessed by my *Cailin das
    donn.*

—o o—

THE EXILE'S LAST TOAST.*

Darkly and coldly in that silent dwelling
The heavy sob burst through the tear-drops
    welling;
Darkly and coldly by that bed of sorrow
She pressed the hand whose touch was froze the
    morrow,
She gazed into those eyes now faintly dimming,
That once with love's soft lustrous light were
    brimming.—

* Founded on an incident taken from Mitchel's lecture
on Thomas Devin Reilly.

She spoke—he heeded not—his cheeks were flushing
With dreams of that green land, whose fervour rushing
Had nerved his soul in youth to front the danger,
To raise his arm and voice against the stranger,
Th' accursèd foe, whose savage might had parted
That land and him, and left him broken-hearted.

But wilder and wilder grew his look,
   And a strange light shone in his eye;
That soft white hand in his clasp he took,
   While his words drowned the bursting sigh:
O love of my heart! I've not long to live,
Yet ere I depart I've a toast to give;
So bring me a bumper of sparkling wine,
'T is the last will flash in this hand of mine.

He raised him from the bed of death,
   And steadied each quivering limb,
And took the cup with a trembling breath,
   And filled it high to the brim.
Then his spirit swept back to the mountains wild,
To the gushing streams and the green wood mild,
To the cabin lone by the swelling river,
Whose tide was *crooning* a sweet song ever;

And he thought of the burning hopes of old,
Of the burnished banner of green and gold,
Of the glowing thoughts and the fearless will,
And the love that no tyrant hand could chill;
And he clutched the sword again in his hand
'Mid the marshalled ranks of his mother-land.
Thus rushed the past through his gallant soul
    With the force and strength of a surging river,
And he kissed the wine in the flowing bowl,
    And pledged: "Old Erin's Isle for ever!"

The goblet fell to earth, he sank again,
    And drew his wife and infant to his breast,—
No sigh escaped—no parting moan of pain;
    His chains were broke—the exile was at rest.

CHRISTMAS SONG.

Brightly the embers are blazing,
    Brightly the festive cups shine;
Round the board soft eyes are gazing,
    Sparkling and radiant as wine.
Faces long pale now are beaming
    With laughter and loving delight;

Clouds long unbroken are gleaming
  With flushes of moonlight to-night.
    Cead mille failte, old Christmas!
      Merrilie dings the wild chime;
    Cead mille failte, old Christmas!
      Hurrah for the brave Christmas time!

Silent the mill-wheel of labour,
  Silent the office and mart—
The soldier has sheathèd his sabre,
  The student is merry at heart.
Over the snow-misted heather
  Cottages mantle with light,
While we sit toasting together
  The pleasures and hopes of the night.
    Cead mille failte, old Christmas!
      Merrilie dings the wild chime;
    Cead mille failte, old Christmas!
      Hurrah for the brave Christmas time!

Here 's to the brave men of Ireland,
  At home, or in exile away;
Here 's to the hopes of our sireland,
  That never will rust in decay.
To every brave, down-trodden nation
  Here 's Liberty, glorious and bright;
But oh! let our country's salvation
  Be toasted the warmest to-night!

Cead mille failte, old Christmas!
Merrilie dings the wild chime;
Cead mille failte, old Christmas!
Hurrah for the brave Christmas time!

—◦◦—

CHARLEY MOR O'DONAHOE.

A BALLAD.

O Charley Mor O'Donahoe,
    I never thought that I
Would find you without home or friends
    Beneath the frosty sky.
I did not dream, ten years ago,
    Beside your cheerful hearth,
Its owner would be forced to roam
    An outcast o'er the earth.

An' where are Shawn and Moran gone?
    Where, where is little Grace,
Whose eyes of blue would brighten up
    The passing traveller's face?
Where is the white house on the hill—
    The cornfields at its back—
That Charley Mor O'Donahoe
    Must take the beggar's track?

The old man placed his long, thin hands
    Upon his trembling knee;
He rubbed the cold frost from his brow,
    And spoke me mournfullie;
Not in the jovial tones of old—
    The wild tongue of the Gael;
But in a broken, husky voice,
    Like a weary mourner's wail.

"Oh! is it you, *avic machree*,
    That I have met at last?
Oh! *wirrasthru!* sure every word
    Recalls the happy past—
The reaping times, the mowing times,
    Where brown streams swiftly flow,
When the lightest hearts were yours and min
    In the valleys of Mayo.

Where is the white house on the hill?
    'T was levelled to the ground
By evil law and ruthless hands,
    And bayonets flashing round.
We could not pay 'my lord' the rent,
    For cold and famine came;
And a hundred roofs, as well as mine,
    Were given to the flame!

And Moran he was far away
  Beyond the western wave,
And Shawn was standing calmly by
  As silent as the grave;
And Gracie clasped the olden post
  That stood beside the door,
Her arms around my swelling neck,
  Till they dragged us from the floor.

The moon was hid in mist that night,
  The freezing snow poured down,
And 'Captain's' howling might be heard
  Far off in Westport town.
Two forms crouched by the bleak wayside,
  Like spectres there alone—
I, with my darling in my arms—
  But where, oh! where was Shawn?

Dawn came. I felt a heavy chill
  Creep through my freezing blood;
I felt a cold hand clutched in mine,
  And raised my *colleen's* hood.
Do n't wonder if my sad heart broke
  And if my reason fled!—
White as the lily of the May,
  My darling child lay dead!

I heeded not the drifting sleet,
  I heeded not the wind,
Nor did I hear a cautious foot
  Advancing from behind.
A warm breath thawed the icy dew
  Upon my senseless brow;—
'Avenged! avenged! a brother's hand
  Fulfilled a brother's vow'.

   *   *   *   *   *   *

Seven weeks she slept beneath the cross—
  Seven weeks her soul was free;
Full brightly rose the April sun—
  The birds sang merrilie.
The streams dashed on with shout and song;
  The breezes laughed in glee;
And Shawn was looking in my face
  Down from the gallows tree.

He shot the landlord at his gate:
  An outlaw on the moor,
They tracked him to his hiding place,
  And chained him fast and sure.
I heard the clicking of a bolt,
  A deep and murm'ring prayer—
A moment, and my bouchal bawn
  Was swinging in the air.

They buried him without a shroud
  Deep in the hilly clay.
We came at midnight's dreary hour,
  And stole his corse away.
We marched by many a lonely road,
  O'er many a moorland wide,
To bear him to his mother's grave,
  And lay them side by side.

As drifts a withered beechen leaf
  Across the lowland plain,
Since then I roved from door to door
  In poverty and pain.
A snow-white face is pressed to mine,
  Wherever I may go;
I hear the clicking of a bolt—
  I feel the heavy snow".

"One is forgotten. Where is he?"
"On Fredericksburgh's grim height
He fell when Meagher's men poured on,
  The vanguard of the fight.
He died like an O'Donahoe,
  His rifle in his grasp,
Old Ireland's name upon his lips
  Unto the latest gasp".

Down by the blazing fire we sat—
  My heart felt drear and lone,
I thought upon brave Hugh O'Neil,
  Poor Emmet, and Wolfe Tone,
And all the gallant efforts made
  To right the dear old land,
But leaving only deeper trace
  Of the Invader's hand.

MAIRE DHU.

Her heart is mine—she told me so
One winter's night a year ago.
"She 'd rather wed her own *spalpeen*,
Than be the haughty Saxon queen".
My coat was rough, my hands were hard,
  And little wealth I had to woo;
But love had greater power than gold
  To win the heart of Maire Dhu.

My love for her I cannot tell—
'T is deep as lone Kilvalley's well,
'T is pure as snow upon the hills,
And gushing as Westmeath's wild rills.

The well shall lose its sainted power,
  The mountain snow shall change its hue,
When Connor's heart will cease to hold
  Thy image there, my Maire Dhu.

Then come, *astor*, and be the light
To make my humble cabin bright,
And poverty's chill woes shall flee
Before thy steps, *gra gal machree*.
They talk of angels from the sky—
  My angel I will find in you;
And sure 't was angels from on high
  That taught that smile to Maire Dhu.

I RAMBLED DOWN THE WOODLAND PATH.

I rambled down the woodland path
  One Sunday evening lately,
    And I met there
    A maiden fair,
A maiden proud and stately;
So beautiful she seemed to me,
My young heart throbbed right joyfully;
I called her my *gra ban machree*,
  That maiden proud and stately.

The May-wind kissed her flowing hair,
  Like summer sun-rays twining,
    And oh! her face
    Of loving grace,
An apple-blossom shining.
Her lips were red as Keenagh's rose,
Her feet as light as mountain doe's,
Her voice the fairy's song which flows
  When starlit eves are shining.

And many a time I've walked that path
  Those Sunday evenings lately,
    Still meeting there
    That maiden fair,
With head erect and stately.
She never gives a smile to me,
But my young heart throbs joyfully,
For she is my *gra ban machree*,
  That maiden proud and stately!

TWILIGHT MUSIC.

The winter moon is shining,
  The pale blue air is still,
A bright-eyed star is peeping
  Beyond lone Ardagh's hill,

And from the far-off distance,
　Across the frosty lea,
A strain of silvery music
　Floats hitherward to me.

How softly, oh! how softly
　The memories wander on
Of faithful hearts long scattered,
　Young friendships dead and gone—
Of eyes of laughing hazel,
　And cheeks of sunny sheen,
The bright love of my boyhood,
　My dark-haired Kathaleen.

A pathway through the woodland
　Lit by the August moon,
The long grass dancing softly,
　The river's whispering tune—
A form beside the trellis,
　Soft lips that welcomed me,
Now resting with the shadows
　Far down beneath the sea.

Float on, sweet twilight music!
　Calm as a meadow stream,
You bear the withered flowers
　Of many a broken dream.

Again the moon shines brightly,
　The sycamores are green,
And I sit beside the doorway
　With dark-haired Kathaleen

ARCHBISHOP HUGHES.

IN MEMORIAM.

A murmur came across the sea,
　On lightning pinions swiftly sped,
From the fair land of liberty—
　"The soldier of the Cross is dead".

From north to south, from east to west,
　Responsive voices sing and sigh,
"We 've given another to the blest—
　Another saint to God on high".

He clasped the shamrock and the cross
　Throughout a long and noble life,
Well may we now lament his loss;
　For who 'll replace him in the strife?

On alien soil, far, far away,
　He ne'er forgot his island green;
Though blessings shone upon his way,
　He sighed for her, the crownless queen.

He blessed her in the matin hymn,
    He blessed her in the vigil prayer,
And saw through vistas cold and dim
    The glory that she yet will wear.

O shepherd Priest! O patriot Saint!
    From thy bright resting-place above
List to the sad and mournful plaint
    That rises from the land you love.

Think of the want and woe and ruin,
    Think of the hearts in bondage vile,
And beg of God to send us soon
    The holy light of Freedom's smile.

KATHALEEN MACHREE.

A<small>IR</small>—*Good night and joy be with you all.*

Oh! sweetly in St. John's old keep
    At midnight sings the fairy choir
Low melodies, that lull to sleep
    The weary peasant by the fire;

And softly as a lover's dream
　　The Shannon wakes a lay for me.
But sweeter, softer still I deem
　　The voice of Kathaleen Machree.

Oh! brightly falls the summer light
　　Upon Roscommon's hills at eve,
And wildly in the witching night
　　Their golden web the moonbeams weave;
And mountain berries cluster fair,
　　And heather bells are sweet to see:
But richer, brighter are the hair
　　And lips of Kathaleen Machree.

Oh! gently now the twilight breeze
　　Wafts fragrance from the meadow side:
But gentler waved the poplar trees
　　The eve she said she 'd be my bride.
How wearily from day to day
　　The lagging moments come and flee!
Ah! how I long for sunny May
　　To wed my Kathaleen Machree!

DONAL KENNY.

"Come, piper, play the 'Shaskan Reel',
   Or else the 'Lasses on the heather',
And, Mary, lay aside your wheel
   Until we dance once more together.
At fair and pattern oft' before
   Of reels and jigs we 've tripped full many;
But ne'er again this loved old floor
   Will feel the foot of Donal Kenny".

Softly she rose and took his hand,
   And softly glided through the measure,
While, clustering round, the village band
   Looked half in sorrow, half in pleasure.
Warm blessings flowed from every lip
   As ceased the dancers' airy motion:
O Blessed Virgin! guide the ship
   Which bears bold Donal o'er the ocean!

"Now God be with you all!" he sighed,
   Adown his face the bright tears flowing—
"God guard you well, *avic*", they cried,
   "Upon the strange path you are going".
So full his breast, he scarce could speak,
   With burning grasp the stretched hands taking,
He pressed a kiss on every cheek,
   And sobbed as if his heart was breaking.

"Boys, don't forget me when I 'm gone,
    For sake of all the days passed over—
The days you spent on heath and bawn,
    With *Donal Ruadh*, the rattlin' rover.
Mary, *agra*, your soft brown eye
    Has willed my fate" (he whispered lowly);
"Another holds thy heart: good bye!
    Heaven grant you both its blessings holy!"

A kiss upon her brow of snow,
    A rush across the moonlit meadow,
Whose broom-clad hazels, trembling slow,
    The mossy boreen wrapped in shadow;
Away o'er Tully's bounding rill,
    And far beyond the Inny river;
One cheer on Carrick's rocky hill,
    And Donal Kenny 's gone for ever.

    *   *   *   *   *   *

The breezes whistled through the sails,
    O'er Galway Bay the ship was heaving,
And smothered groans and bursting wails
    Told all the grief and pain of leaving.
One form among that exiled band
    Of parting sorrow gave no token,
Still was his breath, and cold his hand:
    For Donal Kenny's heart was broken.

I 'M A ROUGH AND READY FELLOW.

I 'm a rough and ready fellow,
    Honest, manly, stout, and true;
What I love, I love for ever;
    What I say I always do;
Never bending bone or sinew
    At the throne of frowning might,
But with hand and heart pulse always
    Banded in the cause of right,
Like a rough and ready fellow
    Working in the cause of right.

I 'm a rough and ready fellow,
    Seldom seen about the town,
But you 'll find me on the mountains
    Far amid the heather brown.
There I own a simple cabin,
    Sitting on the crags above,
Where I live devoid of riches,
    Poor in everything but love,
Like a rough and ready fellow,
    Scarce in everything but love.

When the day's hot work is over
    And the pickaxe thrown aside,
All my toil and care 's forgotten,
    With my children and my bride,

By the hearth we sit together
  As the evening slides along,
Telling quaint old wizard stories,
  Singing bursts of Irish song,
Like a rough and ready fellow,
  Chanting bursts of Irish song.

Hate I give to foreign tyrants,
  Foreign customs, foreign laws;
Love I pledge to dear old Ireland,
  To her glory and her cause.
Through the lonely years I'm waiting,
  Waiting for the promised time
When I'll stand beneath the banner,
  Chorusing the battle chime,
Like a rough and ready fellow,
  Chorusing the battle chime.

MY HOPE.

I've nursed one hope—I've kept it long,
  Outliving all the dreams of childhood,
It haunts me like some old, old song,
  In memories balmed, of rath and wildwood.

Though darkest sorrow fills the heart,
  And steeps the soul in misery,
This cheering hope will ne'er depart—
  My land! that I shall see thee free.

They told me of the faith and truth
  That crowned thy years of ancient glory,
And with the fiery soul of youth
  I pondered on the cherished story,
Until, methought, I saw again
  The tall spears of thy chivalry
Flash from the heather and the glen,
  In sunlit sheen, to make thee free.

Filled with these proud, impulsive dreams,
  I wandered o'er the craggy mountain,
Or musing watched the tinted gleams
  That sparkled from the rushy fountain,
And oft I paced the ruined hall
  Of coulined chief and rapparee—
In fancy striving to recall
  The golden days when thou wert free.

And thus the purpose of my life
  In strength and force was gaining ever—
That burning spirit for the strife
  Of freedom's war—of high endeavour;

Still round my heart these yearnings twine
   As ivy clasps the forest tree—
Still, still I hope, and still I pine,
   My own dear land, to see thee free.

O brothers! let this hope inspire
   Your bosoms too with manly spirit;
Oh, let it fan that sacred fire
   Which men in every clime inherit:
Soul bound to soul—hand clasping hand,
   We'll trample on foul slavery,
And, crowned with glory, take our stand
   Among the noble and the free.

O'SIONACH'S DAUGHTER.

My noble hound! we chase no more
   The deer upon Slieve Galriegh's heather;
Our gallant sport and joy are o'er,
   And here we sit and pine together.
Alas! the day we first did stray
   Down by the Inny's bounding water,
When I beheld that gleaming ray
   Of light and love, O'Sionach's daughter.

The summer radiance, like a bride,
   Now fondly clasps the purple mountain,
And summer breezes ranging wide
   The music bear of bird and fountain;
But nought can soothe my weary heart,
   Since by the Inny's bounding water
Wild love within my breast did start
   For that fair sprite, O'Sionach's daughter.

When others quaff the purple wine,
   Or list the wild harp sounding mellow,
I'm dreaming of her face divine,
   Her soft blue eyes and ringlets yellow:
I'm dreaming of her cabin fair,
   Down by the Inny's bounding water—
Oh! would that I were dwelling there,
   To love and guard O'Sionach's daughter.

My noble hound! my faithful hound,
   You share your master's dreary sadness—
No longer Mornan's woods resound
   The echo of thy bay of gladness;
But at my feet in grief you lie,
   While here I pine for Inny's water,
The silvery tones and laughing eye
   Of that fair sprite, O'Sionach's daughter.

LIVE NOT SLAVES.

"Youth of Ireland, live not slaves".—O'CONNELL.

"Live not slaves, O youth of Ireland!"—
  Thus the mighty Tribune spoke—
"Live not slavish, dastard cravens,
  Cringers 'neath an alien's yoke.
Think upon your famished brethren,
  Think upon your fathers' graves;
By their glories and their sorrows,
  Youth of Ireland, live not slaves!"

"Live not slaves"—this holy teaching
  Is our cherished creed to-day—
Kneel you not to kingly idols—
  Be not worshippers of clay!
For our God has placed within you
  Springs of manliness and truth,
Flashing back in radiant glory,
  All the splendid dreams of youth.

Pathways two fall on your vision—
  One, the rugged path of right;
Soft and flowery is the other
  Course of wrong and golden might;

Over one an angel's winging—
O'er the other fiends of wrath;
Toil and freedom! ease and slavery!
Youth of Ireland, choose your path!

Will ye crouch to silken hirelings?
Will ye bend for gear and gold?
Will ye sell youth's priceless treasure,
Or forsake the faith of old?
Will you part your love of Ireland
For the love of Ireland's foe?
Hark! a million voices pealing,
Fierce as thunder, answer, "No".

Forward, then, and lead the vanguard,
Girt with manliness and truth;
Wrap the sunburst round your bosoms,
In the fervid love of youth:
Forward, then, on freedom's mission,
Over chains and over graves,
And our country shall no longer
Be the dwelling-place of slaves.

IN MEMORIAM.

Rev. John Mulvihill, O.C.C., obiit May 23, 1864.

The bright May sun its radiance shed,
  But nought could penetrate the gloom
  Which settled on that silent room,
Where he, the meek and pure, lay dead.

  A blossom severed from the tree—
    A pillar taken from the dome
    To stand in God's bright happy home,
  In peace and joy eternally.

He fought the fight—he's now at rest:
  Ere half his earthly race was past
  The fetters from his soul he cast—
To sleep upon his Saviour's breast.

The lowly walks of life he trod
  In search of sin and misery,
  To set the slave of Satan free,
And lead the wanderer back to God.

His words unto the heart were balm,
  His hand upraised the fallen one,
  The tempest of the past was gone—
He was the spirit of the calm.

But now the crown is on his brow—
He sees the Mother "full of grace",
The Saviour's mercy-beaming face,
The millions that before Him bow.

Sleep! sleep! our heart's beloved one;
Sleep where the red-breast thrills his lay,
Where fairest bloom the flowers of May—
Sleep, sleep, thy mission here is done.

Sleep while we drop the chilling tear,
The tear of sorrow for thy loss,
Thou faithful bearer of the cross,
Above thy form now resting here.

WATCH AND WAIT.

Watch and wait, boys, watch and wait,
Let it be our motto ever—
Foolish zeal, unguarded hate,
Often baulks a brave endeavour:
God ordains, boys, God ordains,
That we pine a little longer,
Ere we burst the galling chains,
Ere we crush the brutal wronger.

Watch and wait, boys, keep your swords
    Ever flashing sharp and ready,
Heed them not, the scoffer's words—
    Forward, forward, true and steady.
In good time, boys, in good time,
    We shall lift the fallen banner,
And with trust and hope sublime
    March to liberty and honour.

BANNATH LATH.

To P. D——N.

O noble friend! O gallant friend!
God's blessing guard you to the end;
God's wisdom be your guide and stay
On stranger paths in lands away:
This is the prayer of those who see
A brother lost in parting thee.

True was your heart, and brave your hand,
And warm your love for native land;
Your breast a pure and gushing tide
Of Irish love, and Irish pride—
Of Irish trust, and Irish faith,
And purpose changeless until death.

Gone from our vanguard—gone away—
Over the bursting seethiug spray;
Far from the green-encrested hills,
Far from the purple sainted rills—
Gone in the flush of budding years
To join the wide world's pioneers.

O noble friend! O gallant friend!
God's blessing guard you to the end;
God's wisdom be your guide and stay
On stranger paths in lands away.
This is the prayer of those who see
A brother lost in parting thee.

—o o—

COSTELLOE'S LAMENT.

Along the plains of Mayo the wild deer wanders free,
The summer shines in glory, but shineth not for me;
I feel no breeze at twilight, I see no light at dawn,
But I sing a threne of sorrow for my darling Una ban.

The light is quenched for ever in proud M'Donnell's hall,
The harp-song 's hushed all lonely within its towers tall,
The banshee to the brown streams for evermore doth call,
And my true love ne'er shall waken from the cold earth's heavy thrall.

Along the plains of Mayo the wild deer swiftly springs,
Along the plains of Mayo the hunting bugle rings,
My gallant steed is restless, for my strong hand 's on the rein,
But his prancing hoof shall never touch the hunting ground again.

My sword is rusty in its sheath—that blade whose waving glance
Flash'd death to many a lion foe of brave and generous France;
The ribbon from my true love's neck twines round its hilt of gold,
But the snowy hand that placed it there is pulseless now and cold.

I rode in joy and gladness over heathy hill and plain—
I rode in grief and madness on my homeward way again,
For I saw the snow-white rockets tremble coldly in the night,
And my heart grew dark as rainclouds when the stars refuse their light.

I wear within my doublet a bright lock of her hair
That she gave me, when we parted, from her tresses curling fair;
'T is all I have to soothe my woe throughout the coming years—
'T is all I have to bear away the traces of my tears.

Oh! bring me back my own true love, and place her by my side,
As on the harvest evening that I asked her for my bride,
And all the lords of Connaught with their fearless riding men
Would fail to take my darling from my loving arms again.

I 'll get my brave steed ready, and I 'll ride far, far away—
I 'll get my brave steed ready, and ride the livelong day,
Until I find my Una's grave in Kilmacneevan gray,
And pluck a flower from its flowers, and kiss its cold, cold clay.

THE OLD DAYS.

By the Inny's tide I sit while the sun is drooping low,
And I dream a wizard dream of the old days long ago,
When my life was flowing sweet as the merry linnet's song,
Or the " Shrughan" in the glen breathing melodies along.

Then I had a true, true love, and of pleasant friends *go leor*,
And my heart was rich and bright as a mine of silver ore;

I was lightest in the dance—I was swiftest with
the ball,
And my harp and voice were first at the bright-
eyed maiden's call.

'T was the dewy dawn of youth, and my longing
eye could see,
In the days a-coming on, the old banners shining
free;
I could hear the marching clans, and the battle's
fiery strain,
As when Bryan on Clontarf smote to earth the
pirate Dane.

I would gird O'Byrne's sword 'gainst the robbers
of the Pale,
On the field of Beal-ana-buidhe I could charge
with Aodh O'Neil,
Spur upon a moonlight raid with the daring
Rapparee,
Or on Aughrim's deadly plain charge with Sars-
field's chivalry.

But the wintry days are come, and the summer
days are o'er,
And the years are thronging fast round the weary
troubadour;

All my friends are dead and gone, scattered wide
o'er sea and land,
And like to a pillar lone 'mid the ruins now I
stand.

Freedom's battle is unfought—freedom's flag is
folded still,
There is silence in the hall, there is silence on the
hill,
There is rust upon the spear, but the hopes are
still the same,
And the smouldered ashes yet will be kindled
to a flame.

I have strayed for many a day on the sunny soil
of France,
O'er the noble hills of Spain, and where Tiber's
waters glance—
Roving free and roving wild, yet the breath of
every gale
Bore my sighs and my yearnings back to the glens
of Inisfail.

By my native stream again now I sit all lonelily,
My harp and wild old lays all the past has left
to me,

And I hear an angel voice whisper soft as harvest
   rain,
" Sing a song, O minstrel! sing of thy youthful
   days again".

So as the twilight shade steals adown the Shruel
   dells,
I will chant a merry lay to the dancing heather
   bells,
Till the old days and their dreams, like a mine of
   hidden ore,
Come to glad the weary breast of the wand'ring
   troubadour.

KATHALEEN.

A SUN-PICTURE.

Bright lustrous eyes that shed a light
   As soft as sunlight on the meadow;
Black flowing hair and forehead white,
   Like snow wreath 'neath a mountain shadow
Two flushing lips which never part,
   Save when they murmur music airy,
The breathings of a gladsome heart,
   As light and careless as a fairy.

She shines before me like a glance
  Of angel radiance flung from heaven—
She haunts my soul in dreaming trance
  At pale-faced morn and amber even :
Before my spirit ever gleams
  The saintly outline of that vision,
A portrait fair, a gem that seems
  Half born of earth and half elysian.

HOW HAVE YE LABOURED?

As starlight on the sleeping earth
  My early thoughts came to my soul
  That mourned in bitterness and dole,
Of truth and trust the fearful dearth.

I thought of all my early dreams—
  The young hearts marshalled for the fight,
  When Right would march o'er brutal Might,
  And men, in beauty's harness dight,
Quaff flashing draughts of Spartan streams.

When labour strong and proud would raise
  Its sinewed hand to seize the crown,
And loudly chant its marching lays,
  With God's sweet smile a-glancing down.

When blackened walls should cease to pain
The gaze of Christian manhood's eye;
When forms once swept by sleet and rain
By blazing hearths might sit again,
And smile at tempests warring by.

And freemen stand on hill and rock,
　　No master but the Lord above,
　　　And banners long in darkness hid
　　　Shine like a blazing pyramid,
And brethren learn their hearts to lock
　　In the strong clasp of angel love.

All unfulfilled. The earth is dark
　　As ever with the lust of wrong;
Christ's children wander pale and stark
　　Amid the red assassin throng.

And some ask madly, "Where is God?"
　　With boiling veins and streaming eyes,
They blame His justice-dealing rod;
　　They hear no calm voice from the skies:
　　　"How have ye laboured, men of earth,
　　　To win regenerating birth?"

And others whine, with slavish bow,
  "The crowning day will shortly come—
Till then we sit in martyrdom;
Once we had dreams—we spurn them now".
  "How have ye laboured? martyrs, tell",
  Rings out the ceaseless voiceful bell.

And I, too, in my frenzy, held
  Reproachful thoughts, that all my dreams
  Had faded like the four bright streams
Which once in beauteous Eden welled.
  How have you laboured—minstrel, say!—
  To raise your visions from the clay?

"How have you laboured?" This is all,
  O teachers of our fallen land!
To free the stricken one from thrall
  Have ye obeyed the Lord's command
As erst the faithless-hearted Saul,
  Or walked with David and his band?

Ah me! my heart is full of dole—
  The myriads pass with faces white—
I hear a still voice in my soul:
  "Ye did not labour well and true,
  As the appointed men should do
Who lead the strife of truth and right".

AN EXILE'S SONG.

What am I thinking of all the day?
What am I dreaming of all the night?
Why am I sighing when all are gay,
    And gloomy 'mid scenes that are fair and bright?
Answer it, burning and lonely heart!
    Answer it, leagues of ocean foam,
That widely, darkly, and drearily part
    The wandering Celt from his native home!

I was a child in faith and years,
    When I placed my foot on the out-bound ship,
But the tears that trickled were manhood's tears,
    As the sunlit prow in the wave did dip.
The faces grew dim upon the shore,
    And the mountains vanished in mist away,
And a still voice whispered me: "Nevermore
    Shall your eyes look out on your native bay!"

And I thought of Tom, and my brother Ned,
    And Katie, the dearest to me of all;
And I thought of my mother, so cold and dead,
    'Neath the holy shade of the abbey wall;

I thought of the cabin beside the heath,
  Of the daily toil, and the twilight rest,
Till I prayed that the cold, cold hand of death
  Might bear me away to my mother's breast.

'T is twenty years since that bitter day;
  I have learned the sweetness of being free—
But the pulse still beats for the homeward way,
  For the olden loves beyond the sea.
The bright stars shine on my sunbrown face,
  And they find no answering light is there—
No light from the child of a scattered race,
  Save the sickly gleam of a dark despair.

And hopes are whispered in words of flame
  That the days of my country's wrongs shall pass
Full soon away, and the slavish shame
  Be trampled to earth like new-mown grass;
That the scattered shall dwell by their native hearth,
  In their ancient strength and their ancient pride;
That they'll gather from ends of the farthest earth,
  To conquer or die, as their fathers died.

And I dream of this in the silent night,
    And it fills my soul in the open day,
While I fancy the grand and glorious sight
    Of the exiles crossing the homeward way!
But sadness will steal in spite of all,
    And a dim foreboding I ne'er shall see
The mossy side of the abbey wall,
    Or the shining flag of a people free!

Oh! sing me a song of home, true love!
    A ringing song of the brave old times;
And voices will whisper from heaven above
    A soothing tone on the rushing chimes.
Let it bound along on the twilight air,
    Like the charge and tramp of conquering men,
To banish the cloud of my dark despair,
    And light my soul with new hope again!

REVE D' UNE VIE.

Far out upon the heaving sea
    The young moon looks in stillness fair;
And wild and sad and mournfully
    Fresh breezes haunt the autumn air.

All lonely at the window pane
A watcher sits while, one by one,
The scenes of years steal in again,
   Like hues of a departed sun,
     The pictured dreams of olden times,
     Rolled in the light of scattered climes.

Full fifty years, and boyhood's space
   Comes back arrayed in sunsets brown—
The merry songs, the ancient place,
   And gray-arched bridge below the town—
The "inch" girt by the Inny's wave,
   Where sword-leaves hid the wild duck's nest,
The snow-white rock, the fairy's cave,
   The meadows sloping to the west—
     The prayer beside the mother's knee—
     The legends of the *vanithee.*

They enter in from spirit lands,
   As leaves borne on a rushing stream:
He clasps again the friendly hands—
   The loving glances on him beam.
He hears, far o'er the dewy hill,
   The hunting horn's wild melody;
He sees the "hedge-school", where the rill
   Mimicked the schoolboys' careless glee;
     And strays along the violet path
     That circled Creevagh's haunted rath.

O gray old bridge! what shadows slide
  Down from thy battlements so lone!
O home upon the white hill-side,
  Are all thy owners dead and gone?
"Dead, dead and gone", a voice replies
  Low from the cascades' echoed song—
Dead, dead and gone!—but in the skies
  They mingle with the seraph throng;
    One wanderer treads the earthly land
    Of all the loved and loving band.

Weave, weave the web, O memory!
  A dim bark skims the moonlit foam,
And bears to beauteous Italy
  A bright boy from his Irish home.
He stands upon the deck, his eye
  Rests on a stilly western star—
Mo nuar! the yearning heart must fly
  To that sweet resting-spot afar—
    The old white rock, the island brown,
    And bridge of Ballymahon town.

The halls of Rome are grand and fair,
  And flashed with purple light and gold;
But oh! to breathe the summer air
  That blew through Ballymulvey's wold.

All day the weariness and hum,
  But evening brings the vesper chimes,
And all the bursts of feeling come
  That filled the breast in vanished times—
    This memoried spot, life's changeful dream,
    That home beside the Inny's stream.

To pray and labour, work and win,
  And learn God's holy eloquence,
To measure blades with death and sin
  In all the trust of innocence,
To dwell amid the glorious past
  And keep youth's pulses firmly strung,
And hold with memory firm and fast
  The lessons of his earliest tongue—
    So lived the boy till manhood came,
    Crowned with the wreath of truth and fame.

Weave, weave the web, O memory!
  The threads knit closer, one by one:
Again a bright bark skims the sea,
  With prow bent to the setting sun;
The wanderer on the brown deck stands,
  And gazes on the far sea-rim;
He thinks no more of foreign lands—
  That wide expanse holds all for him—
    The star that blossomed in his sky,
    To which his heart would ever fly.

He steps upon his native soil—
Where was the light that filled his years?
Still, still the ceaseless weight of toil,
The prayer, the hope, the lonely tears.
The decades roll in girded space—
Time adds fresh flowers to every grave—
He may not see the olden place,
Or stand beside the olden wave;
　　The Saviour's work must yet be done—
　　The glorious crown is still unwon.

And so, as winds steal from the sea,
And autumn's moon is pacing slow,
All sad and sweet and mournfully
The treasured visions inward flow.
He sits beside the window frame,
And dreams a dream of sunsets brown;
He sees the gray-arched bridge again,
The lonely inch, the silent town,
　　And every fond and loving face
　　That lit life's only resting-place.

DARKNESS.

(AFTER THE GERMAN.)

I bend my head before the shining moon,
   For oh! I cannot look upon its face;
It bears my memory back too soon, too soon
   To the old love—and olden dwelling-place.

I cannot breathe the sweetness of the air—
   That flower perfumed is hanging on my lips;
I cannot look upon the ocean fair
   Where the white gull its homeward pinion dips.

My sorrow s too great for scenes like these;
   Give me the bitterness of death and gloom,
Give me the storm-wind of the icy seas,
   Give me the silence of the grass-grown tomb.

Away, bright eyes! I may not dream of you—
   Oh! shed no light upon my wild despair;
O throbbing heart, thy pulse is beating true—
   Why dream of flowers where every plant's a
      tare?

It is His will, my soul a mausoleum
  Of blighted hopes—the ghosts of things that were—
When will the seal be closed upon the dream?
When will I cease to think of love and her?

THE GRAVE AND THE PRISON.

"Our dead shall be the seed of their decay,
  Our survivors be the shadow of their pride,
Our adversity a dream to pass away,
  Their dishonour a remembrance to abide".
                                    SHELLEY.

Bear ye fresh flowers, O dark-haired maidens,
  Weeping in silence sadly!
Place them around the felon's bier;
Chant his death-song, but drop no tear;
He died in the summer of the year—
  For his love he died full gladly.

Spirits who dwell by freedom's throne—
  The throne of the bright and glorious God—
Waft his soul to your starry zone,
  Far, far, away from the tyrant's rod—
                          Save! oh! save
The doomed of the prison and the grave!

Strong men, brave men of Ireland,
   List to a tale of blood and wrong;
Rest for awhile from your bitter toil,
   And fill your souls with a mourner's song.

He was brave and kind and true,
   Brave and kind as man could be—
Virtue and he together grew,
   Entwined as ivy round a tree.

All that was beautiful and fair,
   He loved with spirit wild and grand—
His native hills, his native air,
   And all in all his native land.

   And she was trodden in the dust,
      And eaten by the cankered sore
      Of fierce oppressors : o'er and o'er
   Her blood-dyed manacles did rust.

Till young blood boiled within the veins,
   And men grew fierce with misery.
   The thousand-banded, column on column,
   Swore with a purpose firm and solemn—
Swore before God to break the chains,
   And set their fallen country free.
   Standing in faith and truth and honour,
   Of the first was he, beneath the banner.

* * * * * *

The bloodhounds loosened from the leash,
    Red bayonets flashing o'er the land,
The arms to lead, the brains to teach,
Clasped in the prison's deadly reach:
Firm as a mass of mountain rock,
Up in the felon-traitor's dock,
    Calmly and proudly he took his stand.

And he was guilty found—
    A traitor to a foreign foe!
Guilt! it was guilt to stop the flow
Of Ireland's stream of toil and wo!
Guilt! it was guilt to right the wrong—
To crush the base and brutal strong,
To make our homes as homes should be,
The dwellings of the pure and free.

Yes, he was guilty; firmly there,
Fronting the judge's coward stare,
With all the hatred of his race
He flung it in each foeman's face,
The die was cast—no hand to save—
The prison first, and then the grave.

Sweetly, sweetly the wild birds sing,
    In the budding leaves by the river Lee—

But faces were pale and hearts were wan
   In a convict ship on the open sea—
Gaily, gaily the young breeze laughed
   With the tones of the twilight bell;
No music can fall on the lonely ear
Save the warder's tramp thro' the windings drear,
Or the muttered hum and the breathing hoarse
Of the forger's sigh and the murderer's curse,
   In an English prison cell.

Sing how starvation cut its way,
Till the spirit burst from its shroud of clay;
Of the dreams that rushed across the soul,
Of the wild, wild pant beyond control,
And the muttered chant of the dismal slave,
"Thy doom is the prison and the grave".

Sing of that dim, and wild, and fearful hour,
   When none were near to whisper one "good-bye",
No sister's eye to pour the dewy shower,
   No brother's clasp to teach him how to die—
Sing, spirits, sing, who watched above his head,
   Whose bright wings closed around his crossless breast,
Tell how the Saviour's Image was denied
   An entrance to that lonely prison bed,

To make his dying hours calm and blest—
Whisper, oh! whisper, how the *assassin* died—
Ruler and priest, with an iron hand
Stamped on his name that hellish brand.

 Miserere—miserere—
  Cold and dead he lies at last;
 Miserere—miserere—
  All his earthly dream is past.
   Let us pray, oh! let us pray,
   He shines in God's bright smile to-day.

 Miserere—miserere—
  Tell the holy rosary;
 Miserere—miserere—
  Chant the prayer from sea to sea,
   That God will save from woe, and dole,
   And agony, the martyr's soul.

Grave his name upon your hearts,
 Tell it to your children too;
Vow, until your life departs,
 Ye and they will be as true—
  True, to the shedding of your blood,
  For hapless Ireland's nationhood.

ST. KILIAN.

A LAY OF THE EARLY MISSIONARY DAYS.

Many a tower and mist-crowned castle standeth
    on thy banks, O Rhine—
Many a legend wingeth onward from that silver
    wave of thine,
Marvels strange, and deeds of glory, wrought by
    peasant, priest, and peer;
So we steal one from thy garland in the dark
    days of the year.
'T was a tall Franconian woodman told this story
    once to me,
As we stood beneath the vine-porch, with the
    corn-moon on the lea,
And I sit beside the hearthstone—wandering
    bard and seanachie,
Chanting forth this golden legend of the time
    when we were free.

I.

Showeth how St. Kilian spent his Infancy.

Nursed beneath an Irish mountain, by an Irish
    mother's hand,
Where the wild Borora whispers to the meadows
    of the land,

Taught the music of the harper and the anthems
of the blest,
Kilian grew as grows the ash-tree by the rivers of
the west.

Winter stars that light in splendour Eire's calm
and solemn sky,
Might have borrowed their chaste brightness from
the gleaming of his eye;
The young lily bending lonely when the dew is
in the air,
Was a type of his meek spirit when his young
lips moved in prayer.

And the angel, who at sunset bore on pearly-
bordered wings
The libations of his spirit upward to the King of
kings,
Whispered in a thrilling whisper to his eager
listening ear,
Dreams of where the nations knew not God, His
teachings, love, or fear.

In his bosom burned a feeling—it was wondrous,
wild, and strange—
On the mission of his Saviour through those far-
off lands to range,

As the autumn sun diffuses light on plain and
    mountain side,
So his lips would breathe the sunlight of Christ's
    Spirit far and wide.

Year on year was gathering o'er him, summers
    came and summers fled,
And they only found him closer to his Master's
    service wed,
And the chieftains clustered round him, and the
    war-clans broke their swords,
For the battle-clouds were scattered at the music
    of his words.

Oh! they sing the fame of Fergus, son of Roy,
    whose silver string
In the halls of proud Emania won the hearts of
    thane and king,
And they tell of glorious Niall, and his knights
    so fierce and tall;
But the Saviour's humble servant in his cell sur-
    passed them all.

II.

Showeth how St. Kilian sailed to Iona and thence to Gaul on his mission.

Shooting on by lonely Rathlin skims a currach on
    the sea,

And it shineth like a snow-flake when the green
    is on the lea,
Rests a bird with crest engoldened where the
    wind-gusts gently stream—
'T is the angel-pilot watching the fulfilment of a
    dream.

And there sit within the vessel, with their faces
    to the land,
Long white beards and eyes of beauty, looking
    back—a silent band;
From the green hills of their country, fairy streams
    and mountains gray,
On the service of their Master they are voyaging
    away.

" Farewell—farewell to Eire—Lord, Thy will be
    done on earth",
Sang they to the shining billow, with celestial
    voice of mirth;
But their brows grew white as marble, and a sad-
    ness filled their song,
As they heard no more the voices in the hallowed
    walls of Cong.

Tarried they in fair Iona till they broke the
    blessed bread,

And their Master's holy benison was poured upon
   each head—
Then St. Kilian led the seapath to the shores of
   beauteous Gaul,
Where they sang a proud *Te Deum*, free from
   sinful care or thrall.

Did he think of lordly Mullagh, or Borora's brown-
   eyed stream,
Of the bright days of his childhood, and his
   country's sunny gleam?
No, he saw but far Franconia, with its skies of
   tesseled blue,
And the crown and palm his bosom was a-yearn-
   ever to.

III.

Showeth, after the conversion of Duke Gosbert and his subjects, how the Saint appeared at a feast to warn him of the sins committed by him through his Queen, Geilana.

Lemoned with the twilight glory, stretched the
   mountains west and east,
And Duke Gosbert and his nobles sat before the
   kingly feast.
They had learned the name of Jesus—they had
   bent the mail-clad knee,
At the soft words of the strangers who had come
   across the sea.

Danced a bright smile o'er their faces, as the
  proud and dark-eyed queen
Bent her arm to lift the goblet glistening o'er
  in jewelled sheen,
And the shouts arose as billows heave above the
  driving ships,
When she pledged her lord and master with the
  red wine to her lips.

But the red wine was untasted, and the soft
  cheeks lost their blood,
For before her in the door-way the Apostle
  calmly stood;
Back he flung his hooded mantle, raised his hand,
  and sternly spoke,
"Thou 'rt not Gosbert's *wife*—Geilana! and this
  union must be broke.

"Prince! upon thy noble forehead the baptismal
  waters fell,
Shall the dark eyes of a woman lead thy footsteps
  down to Hell?
Wilt thou sacrifice the glory that awaiteth thee
  above,
For the poor and fleeting pleasure of a false and
  earthly love?

"Not in anger, but in mercy, doth the Lord look
    down on all;
Bow in sorrow, O Geilana! as Magdalen weep
    thy fall.
Thou shalt like unto the flower withered in the
    freezing snow,
When the April sunbeams woo it, burst anew to
    youthful glow".

Rose up Gosbert, and above him whirled his
    deadly flashing blade,
" On to-morrow, God of Battles, I invoke thy po-
    tent aid—
On to-morrow, ere the mountains feel the last kiss
    of the sun,
If I conquer, what thy servant, Kilian, sayeth
    shall be done.

"Since a youth of beardless visage, when I first
    girt on my sword,
None can say in camp or castle that I ever broke
    my word.
Now thy blessing, holy Kilian"—and they knelt
    down one by one,
While Geilana, brooding vengeance, from the
    banquet hall was gone.

IV.

Showeth how St. Kilian was martyred at Geilana's instigation.

'T was the midnight hour that found them kneeling at the sacred shrine,
Kilian and his companions, hallowed with a light divine;
Wandered back his memory's pulses to the lonely Breffni glen,
And the mountain and the river he was ne'er to see again.

Fluttered past him in the darkness with the gold-encrested head,
The sweet bird whose dulcet music ever charmed his nightly bed,
'T was the signal that the hour of his boyhood's dream was nigh,
When his head would wear the nimbus of the martyred ones on high.

Hush! to-night we break for ever through the dark earth's chilly bars;
Make you ready, for the angels trace a pathway through the stars.

Shone a bright streak in the darkness, and the red assassin's hand
Pierced the pure breasts of St. Kilian, and the chosen of his band!

So they fell before the altar at their loving Master's feet,
With their brethren watching eagerly their coming home to greet,
And the morning found them lying, faces turned to the sky,
Telling truly how St. Patrick taught his followers to die!

And the heart whose deadly passion edged the keen and savage blade,
Burst in madness as an earthquake tearing through a forest glade,
For Geilana wandered wildly o'er the country far and wide,
With the maniac brand upon her, till, by Heaven accursed, she died.

How St. Kilian's name was honoured in the mystic German land,
How the pilgrim read his history in cathedrals tall and grand,

Sung the silvery bells of Wurtzburg in a peal
of melody,
Through the blue mist of the twilight as this tale
was told to me.

V.

What the bard beholdeth in the birth-place of St. Kilian.

Home again—in noble Breffni—filled with yearn-
ings of the past,
Stood I on the Mullagh mountain as the sun's last
line was cast,
And I thought upon the evening far away in
Germany,
When my ears drank in the story which the
woodman told to me.

Upward rose a peal of music: 't was the *angelus*
was sung,
And my pulse was thrilling wildly at the bell's
celestial tongue;
For the dreams of years of childhood came upon
my heart again,
And the wanderer's heart was soothed by the
calm and silvery strain.

'T was a fairy land of echoes, for full many a
league around

Swelled that song in strains responsive to the
    first awakening sound,
And like purple clouds in summer gathering
    round the mountain's crest,
So the past with all its memories closed around
    my saddened breast.

Is that Wurtzburg's shining tower? Do I stand
    on Celtic soil?
Yonder church was built, good minstrel, by the
    lowly sons of toil.
'T was the Mullagh peasants' sinew raised on
    high that beauteous pile,
That the bright eyes of Saint Kilian on his home
    might ever smile.

"Blessings on them", then I answered; "God be
    thanked, the brave old race
In the pathway of their fathers hold the same
    unchanging place,—
Here Saint Kilian's memory dwelleth by Borora's
    brown-eyed rill,
As if foreign banner never floated on an Irish
    hill".

Ye who 've wandered in my footsteps through
    this legend brave and old,

Help ye, as a brother helpeth, with your blessing,
strength, and gold—
Help ye those who rear this trophy through the
ages to live on,
Telling of the martyr's glory when the minstrel's
lay is gone.

THE LADY NUALA'S MEMORIAL.

A.D. 1474.

(INSCRIBED TO C. P. M.)

[See the beautiful papers, "Noctes Lovanienses", from the pen of the Rev. C. P. Meehan, M.R.I.A., in the first series of Duffy's *Hibernian Magazine*, for the materials on which this poem is written. I may observe that to those who wish to get information on a very stirring period of Irish history, those papers are invaluable, and show the research and ability for which the author of the *Confederation* is justly celebrated.]

Why rides the Lady Nuala o'er Galway's pleasant
plain,
With such a host of galloglach and kerne in her
train,
And beauteous ladyes shining in the costly silks
of Spain?

The fathers of St. Francis in Rossriel cloisters
sate,

And they pondered on the sanctity and fervour
 of their state,
When they saw a gallant companie ride towards
 the Abbey gate.

The sun flashed from the bright catbharrs and
 harness dight with gold,
And spear-points thick as hazel stems within a
 mountain wold,
And a lovely ladye led them on, like Judith
 famed of old.

"Oh! tell us, noble ladye, what brings this host-
 ing here?
Why gleam upon this holy spot the deadly sword
 and spear?
None but Francis' blessed children 'neath our
 peaceful roof appear".

"O holy father, we have come the bearers of a
 prayer,
Over many a rugged mountain and valley rich
 and fair,
To thy brethren who in cloistered cell thy found-
 er's habit wear.

I am Ladye Nuala, the wife of Hugh O'Donnell
 Roe,

Whose banner waves where silvery Esk and
murmuring Erne flow;
Where the Saints of God lived, prayed, and died
in days of long ago.

And they planted there a garden of sweetest
scent and hue,
Till the tempest came, and from its wings a poi-
soning shadow threw,
And the weeds are now grown strong and rank
—the flowers are only few.

"So come, O blessed father, and cast wide the
seed again
That Saint Patrick brought unto our shores
across the white-browed main,
And our Saviour watered with His Blood in
agonie and pain.

"And the vesper hymn will rise once more be-
side our winding bay,
As the red sun steals beneath the waves to gol-
den lands away,
And the white stars, like The Virgin's eyes,
smile on the headlands gray.

"Oh! come and gather in thy flock from clifted
shore and hill,

And teach Tirconnell's gallant sons their Heavenly Master's will,
And His blessing, like a moonlit mist, will rest above us still ".

Thus answered then the father this noble lady's prayer :
" It pains us that unto your land we cannot now repair.
Some future time, with God's good grace, we 'll turn our footsteps there ".

Deep sorrow darkened on the brow of galloglach and kerne,
And the maiden faces drooped as droops the rain-washed island fern,
Till the ladye raised her hand, and spoke in angry tones and stern :

" Then beware th' avenging wrath of God,—for every soul that 's lost ;
Let it be for once and ever at your peril and your cost".
" Amen " rose wild and solemn from the white lips of the host.

Out the friars, through the open gate, came one, and two, and three,

Till they stood within the centre of the noble
companie—
"We of our number, ladye, will gladly follow
thee".

Oh! sweetly, sweetly did she smile and cast to
heaven her eyes,
To thank the Lord for blessing thus her saintly
enterprise,
And a shout of gladness echoed to the laughing
summer skies.

So the joyful cohort travelled on their spreading
distant way,
Over rugged hills and valleys fair for many and
many a day,
Till the sea-wind kissed their weary brows by
Donegal's wild bay.

And thus the Lady Nuala, with her noble chief-
tains all,
Raised the Abbey of St. Francis by the waves of
Donegal—
Christ save her chaste and loving soul from Pur-
gatorial thrall!

THE BURNING OF DONEGAL ABBEY.

[See Note.]

PART I.

O'Donnell was down in Thomond,
  With his chiefs and clansmen all,
And many an anxious hour we passed,
With Mass, and hymn, and holy fast,
  In the abbey of Donegal,
Praying the Lord from His throne afar
To keep from our walls the flame of war.

But onward came the tidings
  By trusty *asklas* borne—
That Nial Garve O'Donnell's clan
Were mustered to a single man
  In Saxon fealty sworn:
The country wide was now their prey,
Nor home, nor sacred shrine spared they.

Then rose up from our brethren
  A wail of bitter woe,
How could they leave the sacred spot,
Where worldly cares intruded not,
  Poor wanderers forth to go;

Out on a world of crime and sin,
To mingle with its clang and din?

We placed the sacred vessels
　In a good ship on the bay,
For we saw the craven traitor's flag,—
The blood-red flare of the Saxon rag,
　On the hill-paths far away—
Then forth we went and bid farewell
To altar, and shrine, and holy cell.

It was upon St. Lawrence eve,
　From the gray woods at the east,
The traitor clansmen poured along,
With savage jest and ribald song
　Accursed of monk and priest;
Soon in our abbey's holy shade
Tramped the spearmen of the renegade.

Then we prayed to good St. Francis,
　In each lonely hiding place
(Which the mountain wolf alone could track),
That God might send our chieftain back
　As the saviour of his race;
For we knew the strength of his fiery sword
Would scatter the base defiling horde.

And ever, ever southward
  We turned our weary eyes,
While Saxon cannon firmly lined
The abbey front and far behind
  With caution keen and wise;
Their muskets o'er the ramparts shone,
Flashing beneath the August sun.

PART II.

The gray clouds floated eastwards,
  The sunlight kissed the strand,
And down from Carrig wild and free
Rush Hugh O'Donnell's chivalry,
  A brave unconquered band—
Pale grew the traitor Nial then—
And quailed the hearts of all his men.

Out from the walls looked veterans
  In myriad battles tried—
Men who had fought at Clontibret
Until the star of Norris set,
  And stood where Bagnal died—
Yet those stout hearts were troubled sore
That never quailed at foe before.

And round and round, a circle,
  Like a red belt of fire,

Clasps the doomed fort; while, pent within,
God's shrine beheld the Saxon's sin.
   Now nigher, ever nigher,
Advance the leaguers—gun to gun,
The thick smoke hides the blazing sun.

It was the eve of Michaelmas
   Beside the Erne I stood,
My brethren all were wrapt in prayer
While I stood calmly watching there
   That fearful scene of blood—
The spring breeze swept up from the sea,
And whistled onward merrilie.

" O God! hast Thou deserted us?"
   In my anguish thus I said;
Christ save us! what a fearful glare,
What a thundering crash swept thro' the air!
   Heaven's bolt at length has sped;
Upward a fiery demon tore—
'T is the powder sprung from the chancel floor.

And far and wide the echoes
   Told forth the cry of death—
(Ah me! that dark and fearful day!)
Under the blazing ruins lay,
   For many a foot beneath,

The invaders of the sanctuary :—
Woe, woe for them in days to be.

*   *   *   *   *

Dark Nial in London's Tower died
    With the Cain mark on his brow;
And far away, far, far away,
In Valladolid's cloisters gray,
    Sleeps Hugh O'Donnell now :
Hugh the undaunted, gallant Hugh,
To faith and country ever TRUE.

The sun smiled on the mountains,
    The young breeze kissed the strand;
But ne'er again the vesper call
Was heard within the abbey wall.
    A ruin in the land—
It stands, unchangeable as death,
The emblem of a changeless faith.

I, Donough the monk, now tell this tale,
As the white snow moves from the rising gale.

MY CAILIN RUADH.

My fairy girl, my darling girl,
   If I were near thee now,
The sunlight of your eyes would chase
   The sorrow from my brow;
Your lips would whisper o'er and o'er
   The words so fond and true,
They whispered long and long ago,
   My gentle Cailin Ruadh.

No more by Inny's bank I sit,
   Or rove the meadows brown,
But count the weary hours away
   Pent in this dismal town;
I cannot breathe the pasture air,
   My father's homestead view,
Or see another face like thine,
   My gentle Cailin Ruadh.

Thy laugh was like the echo sent
   From Oonagh's crystal hall;
Thy eyes the moonlight's flashing glance
   Upon a waterfall;

Thy hair the amber clouds at eve,
    When lovers haste to woo;
Thy teeth Killarney's snowy pearls,
    My gentle Cailin Ruadh.

O sweetheart! I can see thee stand
    Beside the orchard stile,
The dawn upon thy regal brow,
    Upon thy mouth a smile;
The apple-bloom above thy head,
    Thy cheeks its glowing hue,
The sunflash in thy radiant eyes,
    My gentle Cailin Ruadh.

But drearily and wearily
    The snow is drifting by,
And drearily and wearily
    It bears my lonely sigh
Far from this lonely Connaught town,
    To Inny's wave of blue,
To the homestead in the fairy glen,
    And gentle Cailin Ruadh.

TO PROFESSOR J. W. GLOVER.

Wake up the harp of him* who lowly sleeps,
  Balmed in the dew of Ireland's silent tears;
Teach us to weep whene'er the minstrel weeps;
  Teach us the glory of the olden years,
  When Ireland stood the peerless among peers;
Strike the wild march where high on Knockninoss
  Colkitto stood among his broken clan,
When Saxon blood flowed darkly on the moss
  Till evening's moon was rising sad and wan,
  And breezes came to mourn the heroes gone.
Then let our souls be borne athrough the mist
  Of ages past, when he,† the minstrel, fell,
Or conquering Brian marched, and, as we list,
  We hear the kingly conflict, and the knell
That speaks of vanished days, when o'er the land
Soft harps were touched, as thine, by wizard hand.
Wake up those memories of the glorious past,
And linked with his thy name shall ever last.

    * Moore.   † The Minstrel Boy.

L' ENVOI.

I 've twined the last leaf of my garland,
    The night clouds are darkening the sky,
And a voice from the gray dusk is whispering —
    "O minstrel, good bye!"

Soft music is filling the silence,
    Eyes glance like the eyes of the dead;
But the music dies out thro' the casement,
    The bright eyes are fled.

I 've twined the last leaf of my garland;
    A lonely star shines in the sky,
And the heart of the poet is weary:
    O bright eyes! good bye.

FINIS.

NOTES.

I.
The Burning of Donegal.

In the *Noctes Lovanienses*, written by my esteemed friend, Rev. C. P. Meehan, and published in Duffy's *Hibernian Magazine* (old series), a full account of the burning of this once famous abbey will be found, to which the reader is referred for the materials on which the ballad is written.

II.
The Grave and the Prison.

Few who have read the report of John Lynch's trial at the Cork special commission, for Fenianism, and his letter to his sweetheart, Miss Nunan, but will forget their political predilections, and sympathise with the unfortunate fellow, whose fate has been so well described in Mr. Hennessy's paper on political prisoners. I have merely written what I would write were the victim a native of any other country, instead of being an Irishman.

www.ingramcontent.com/pod-product-compliance
Lightning Source LLC
Chambersburg PA
CBHW031501160426
43195CB00010BB/1053